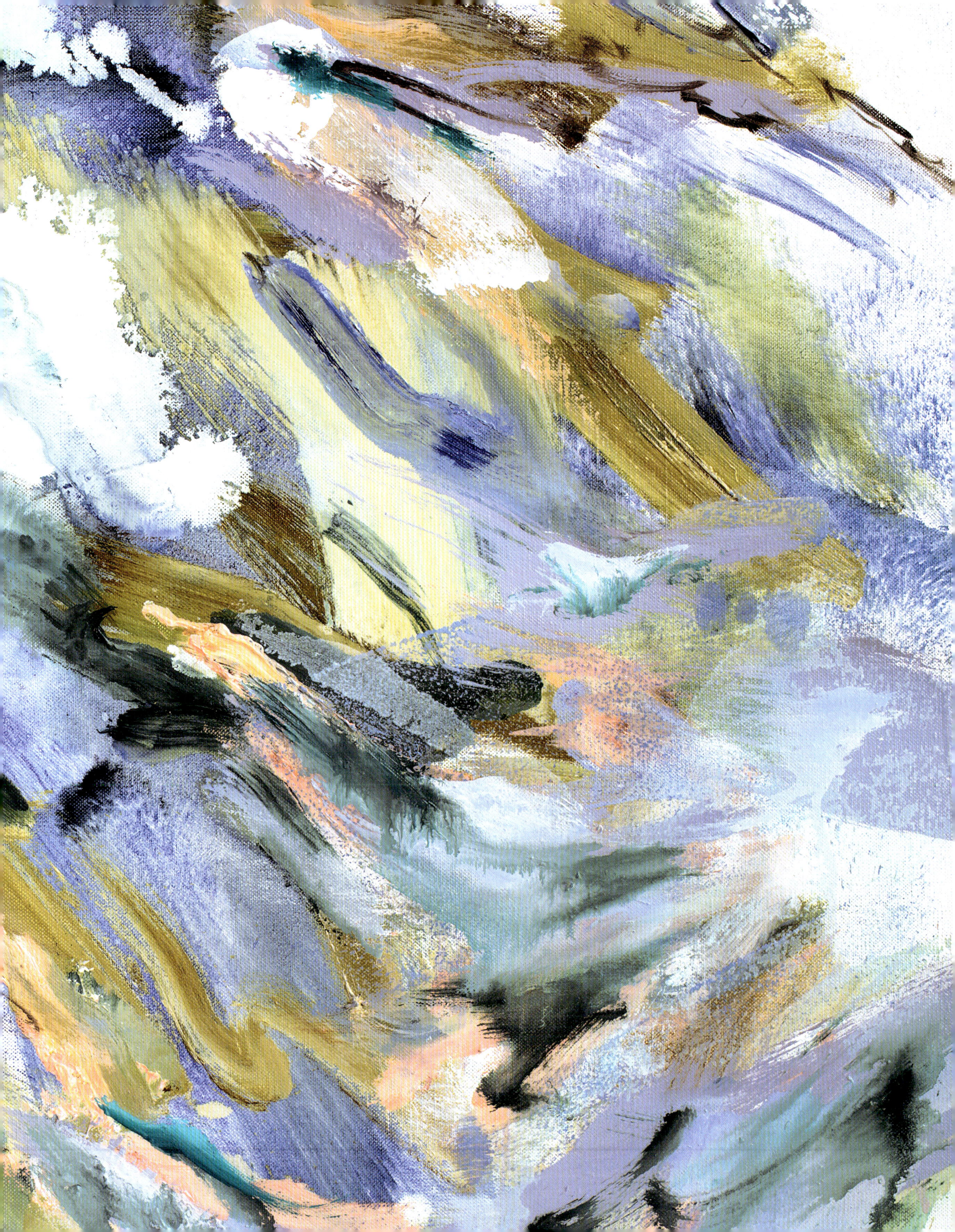

Kylie Manning

Contents

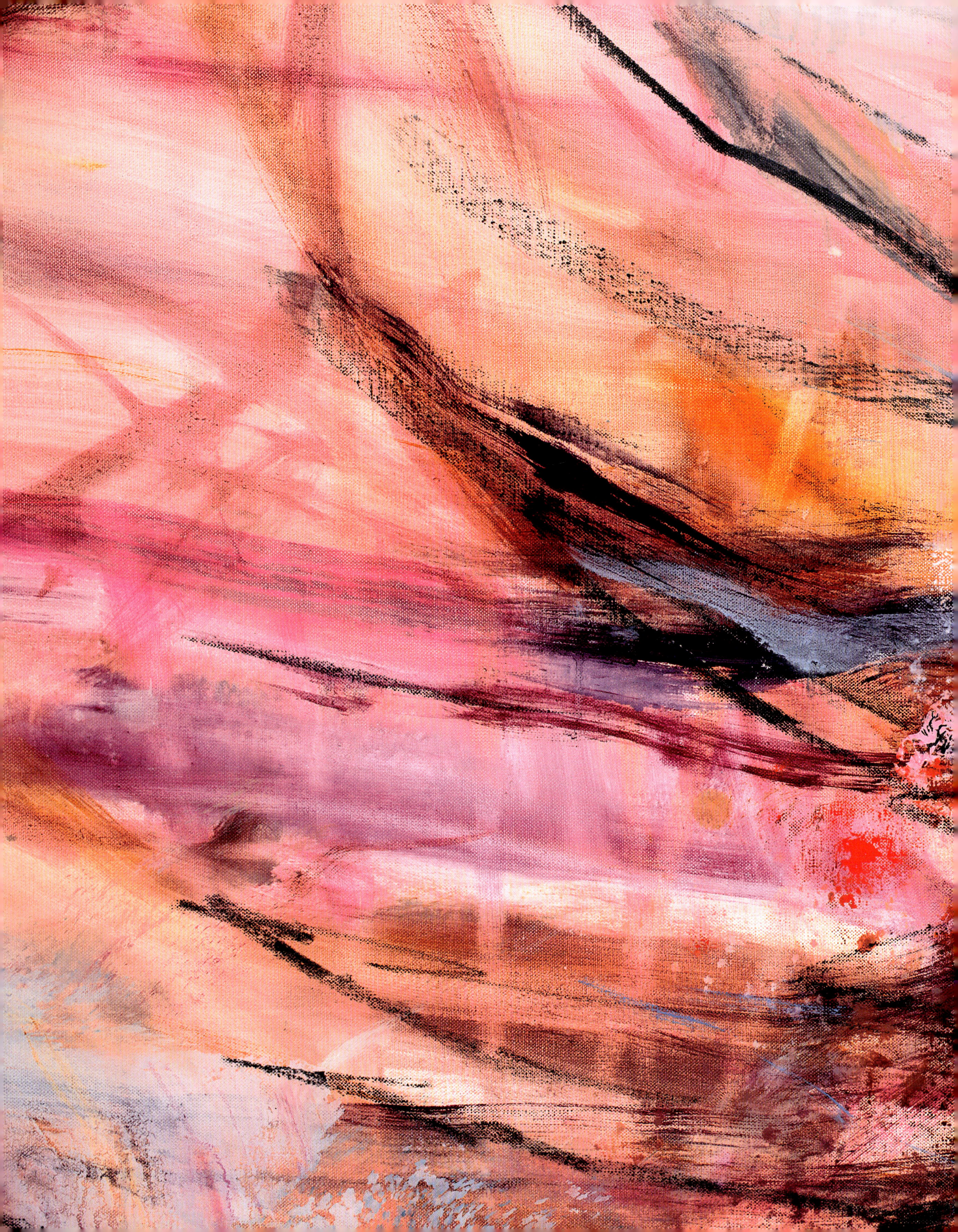

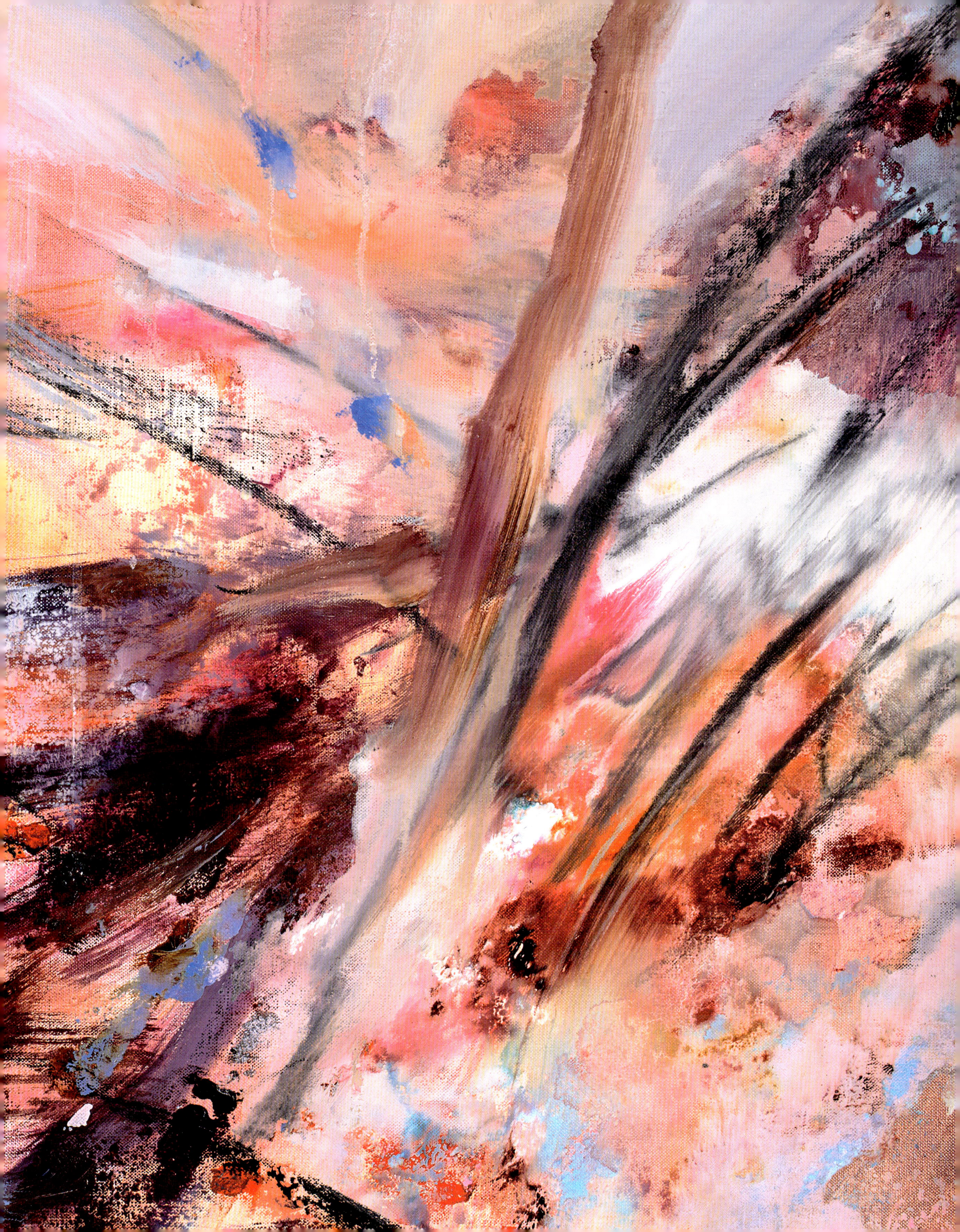

Jetsam
2023
oil on linen
70 × 90" | 177.8 × 228.6 cm

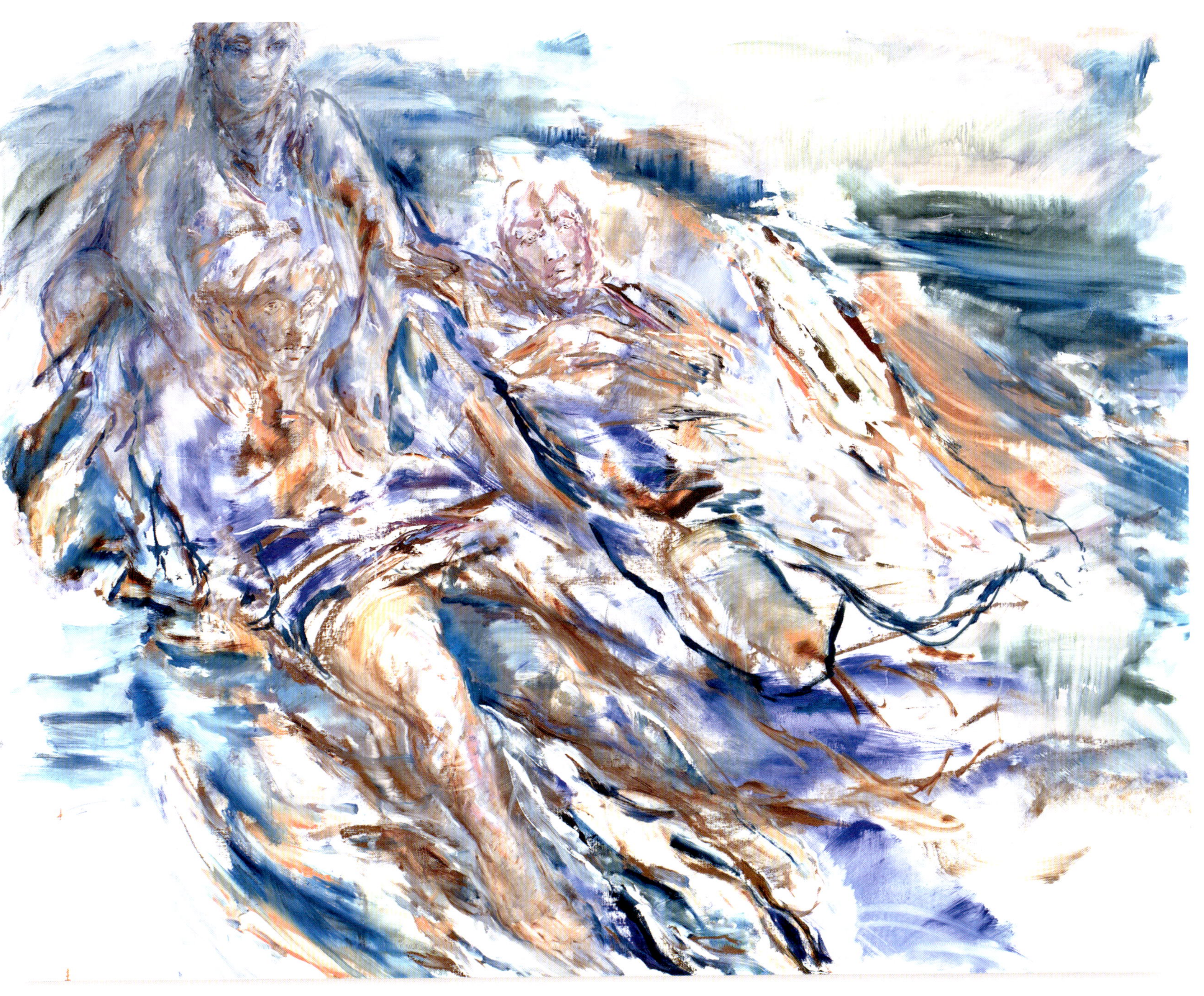

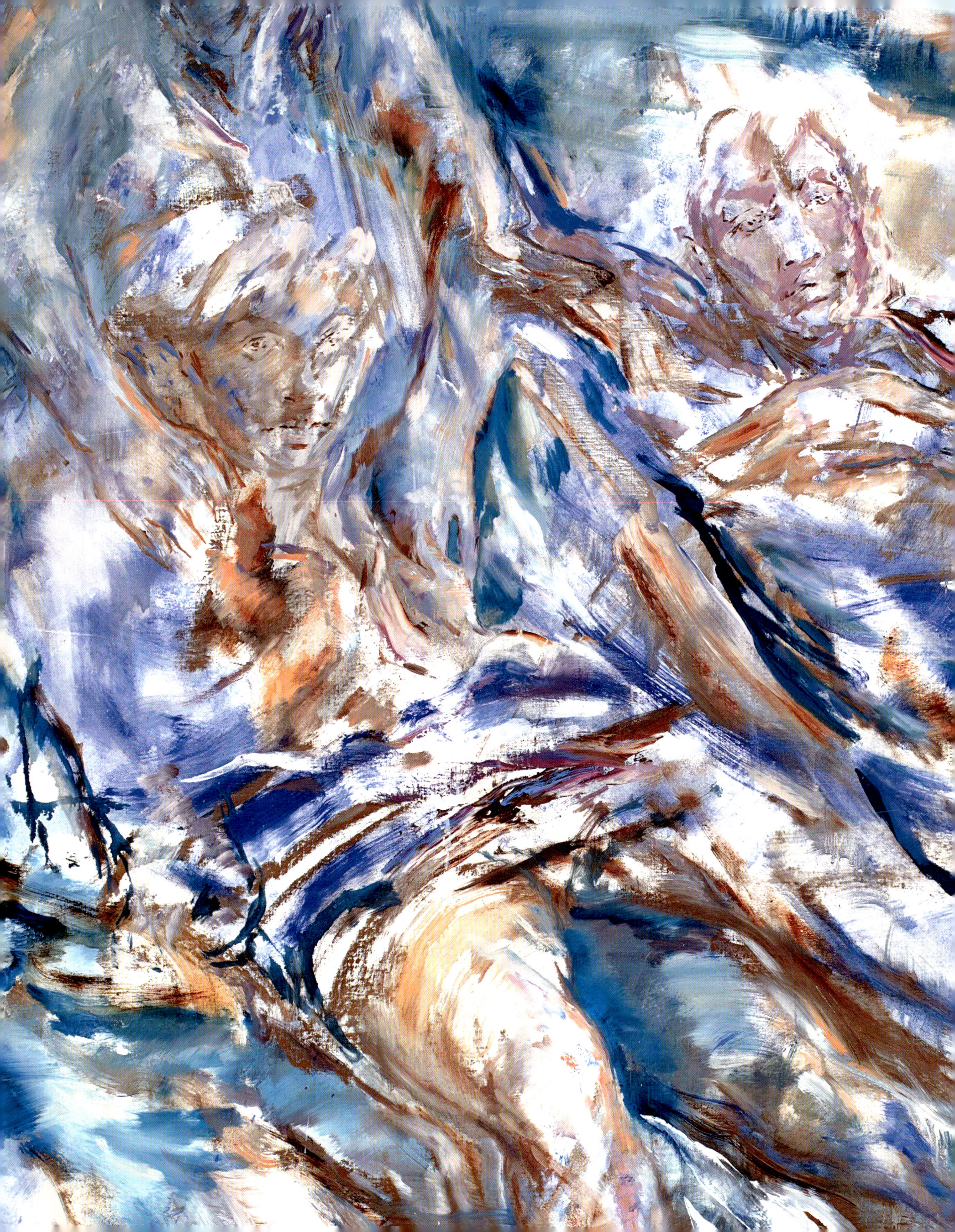

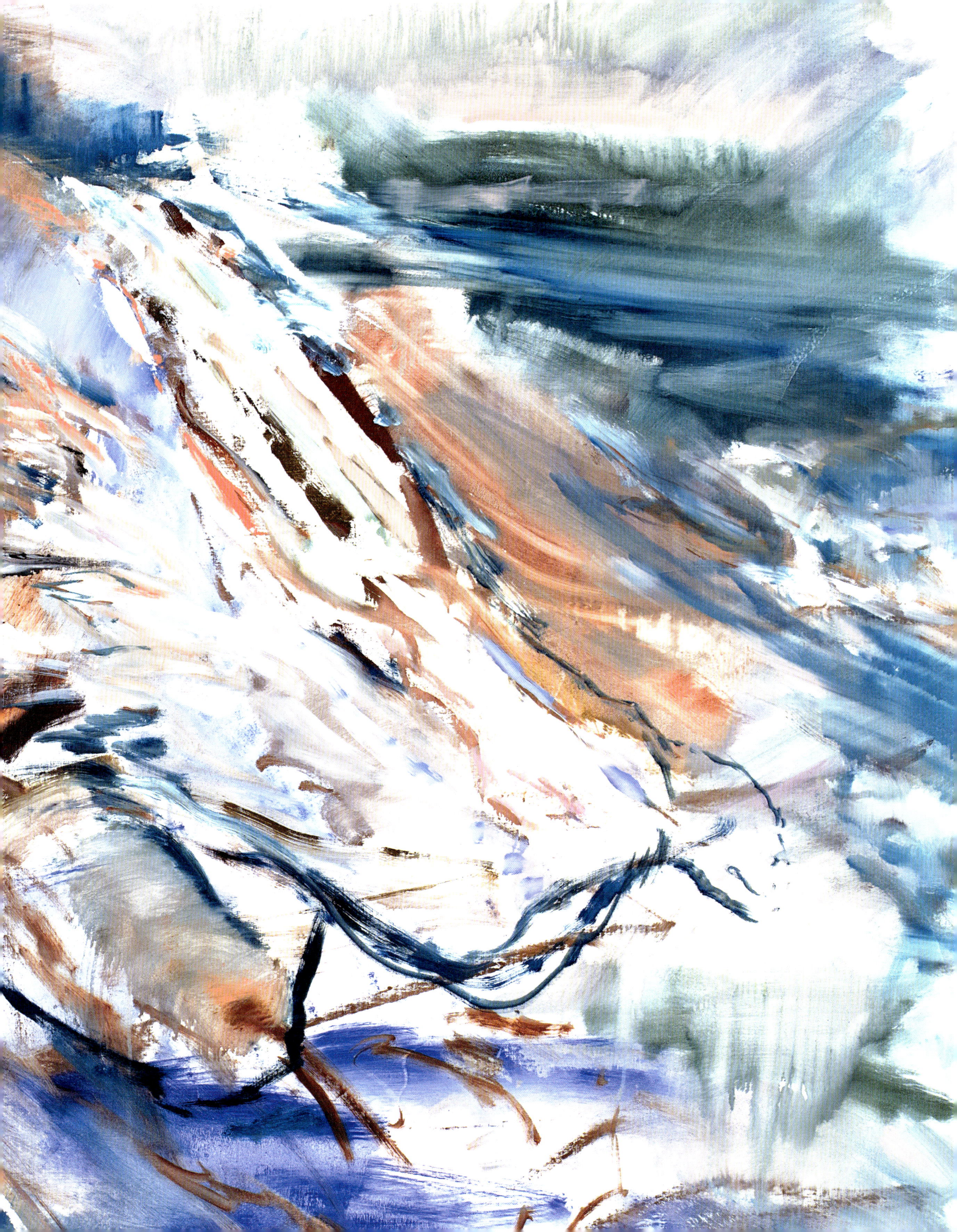

Hold on Tight
2021
oil on linen
60×72" | 152.4×182.9 cm

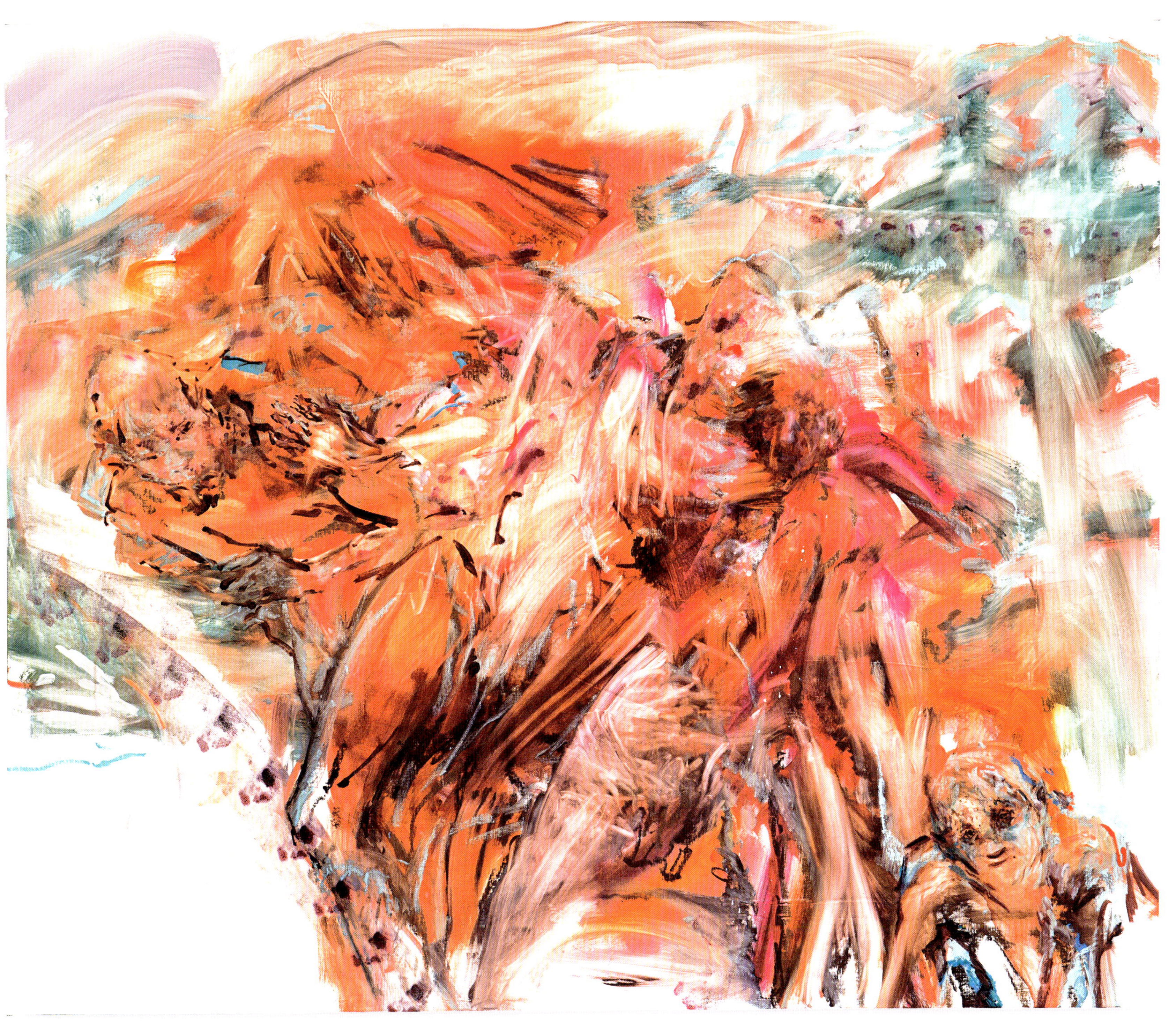

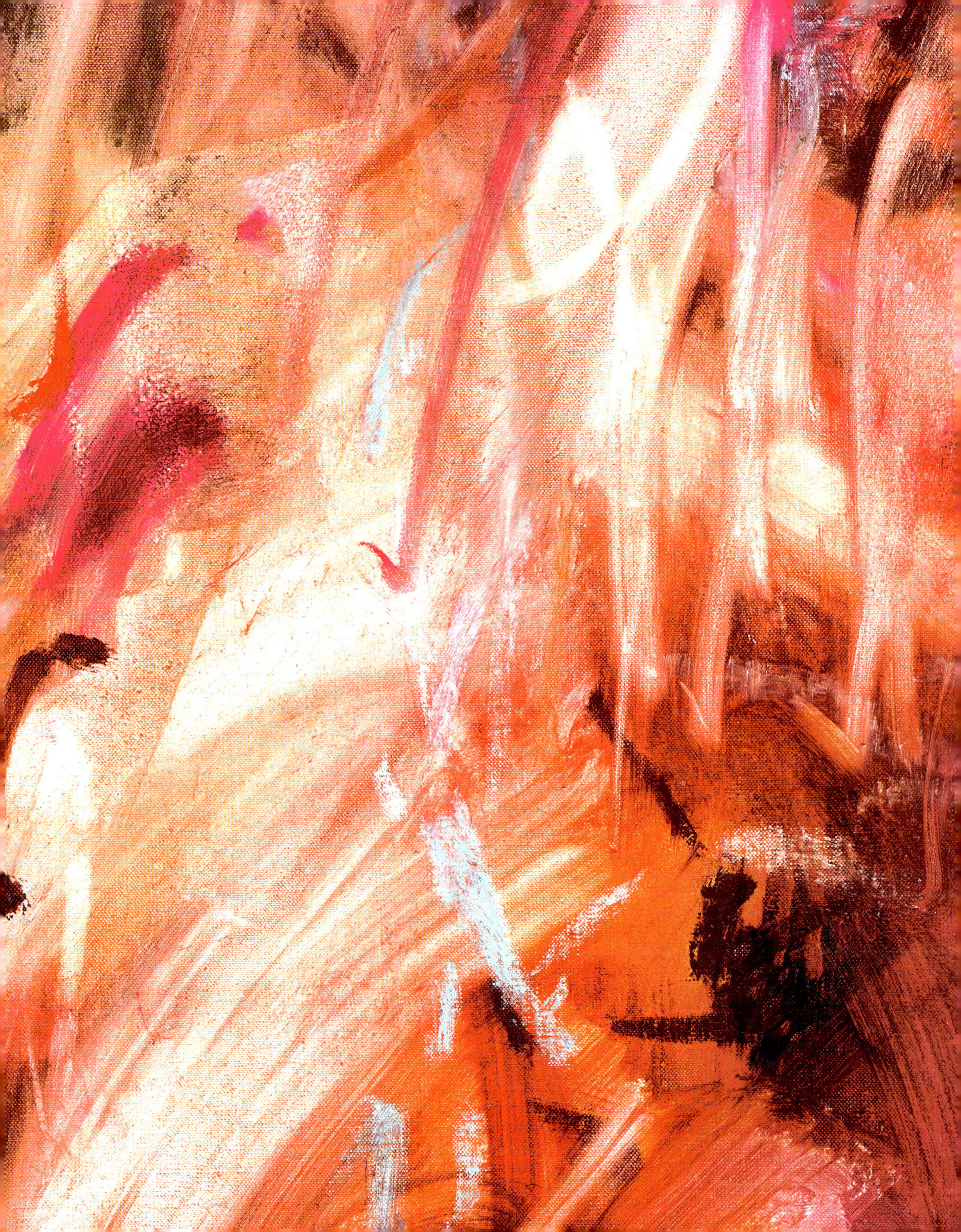

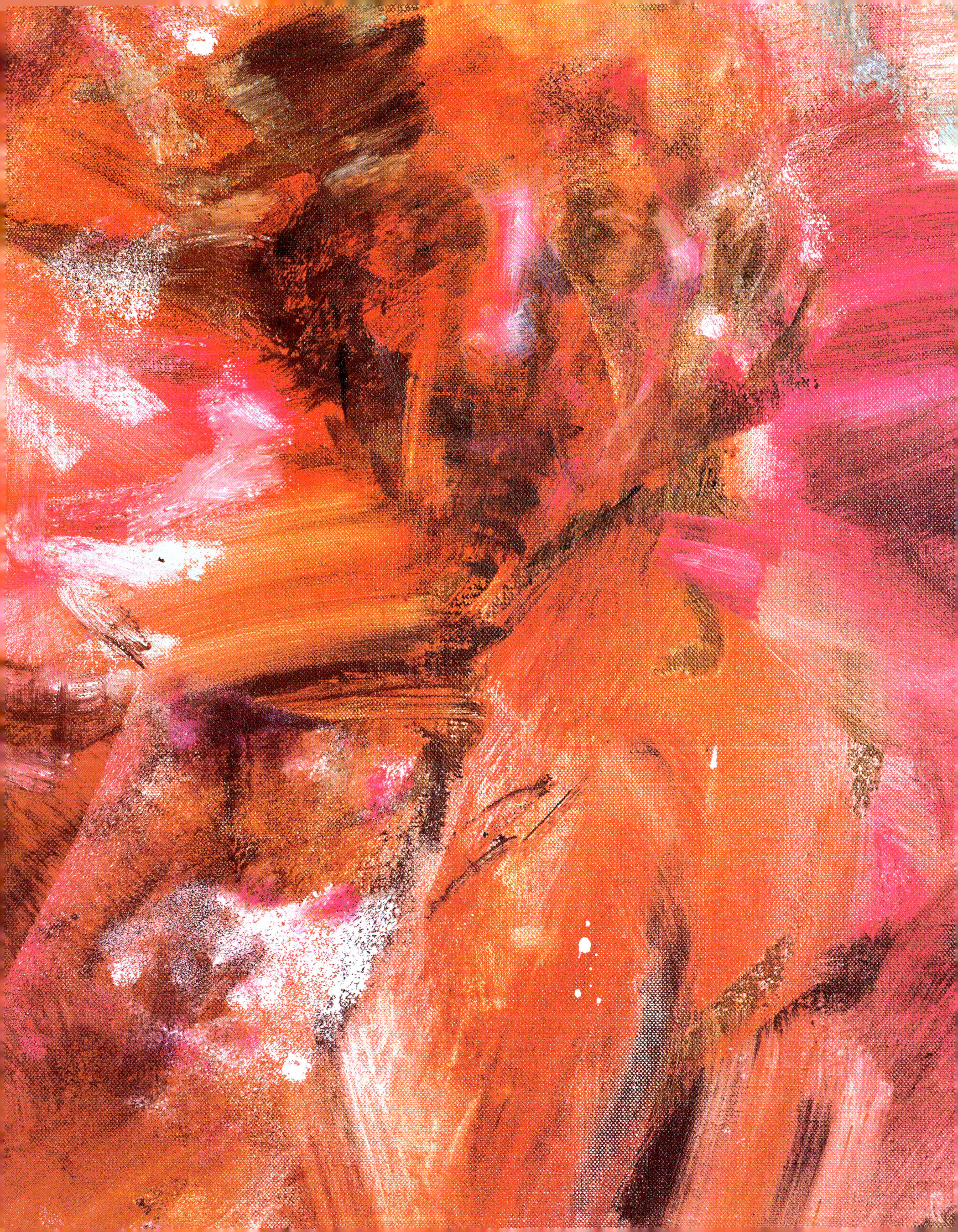

Undertow
2023
oil on linen
70 × 90" | 177.8 × 228.6 cm

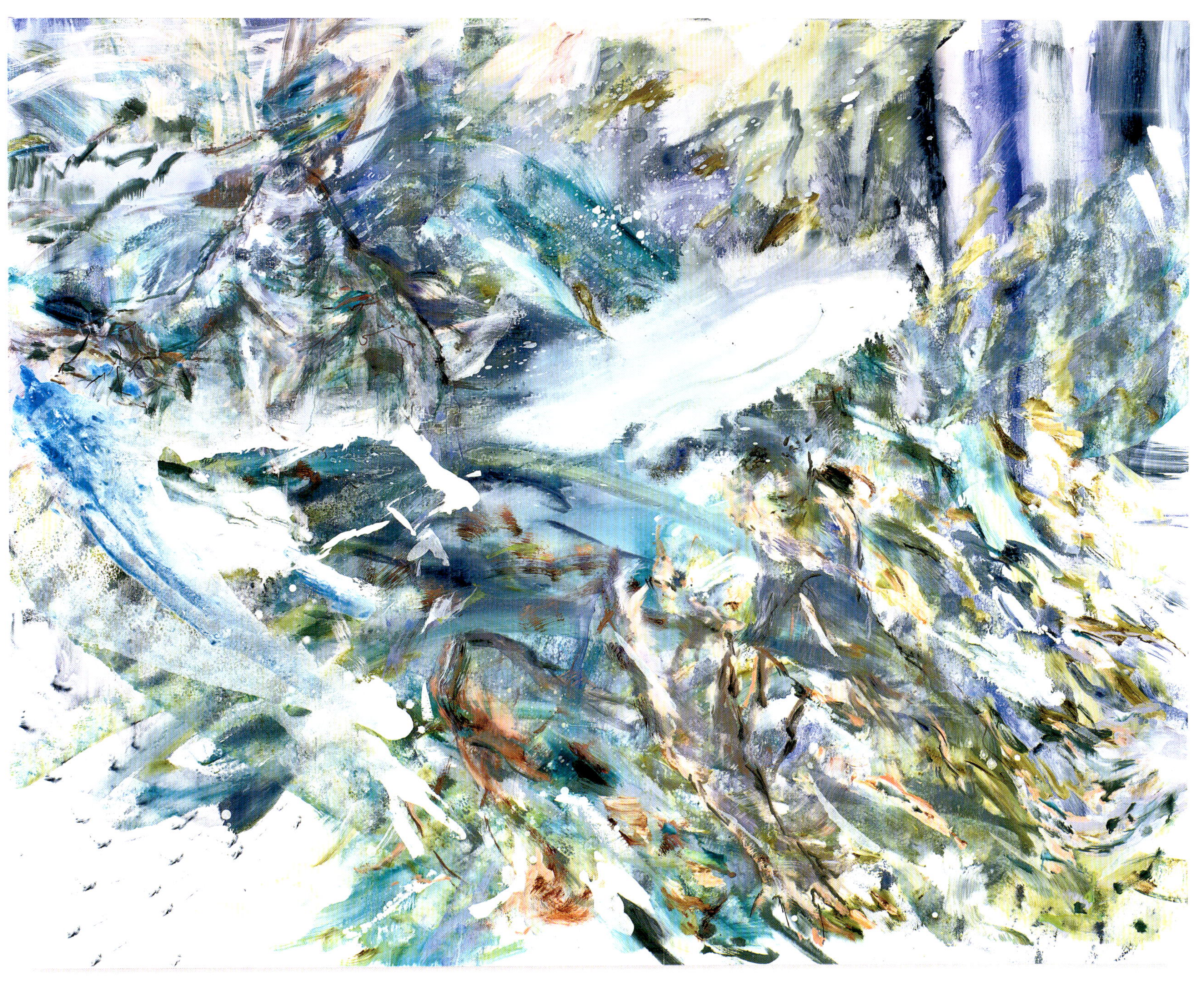

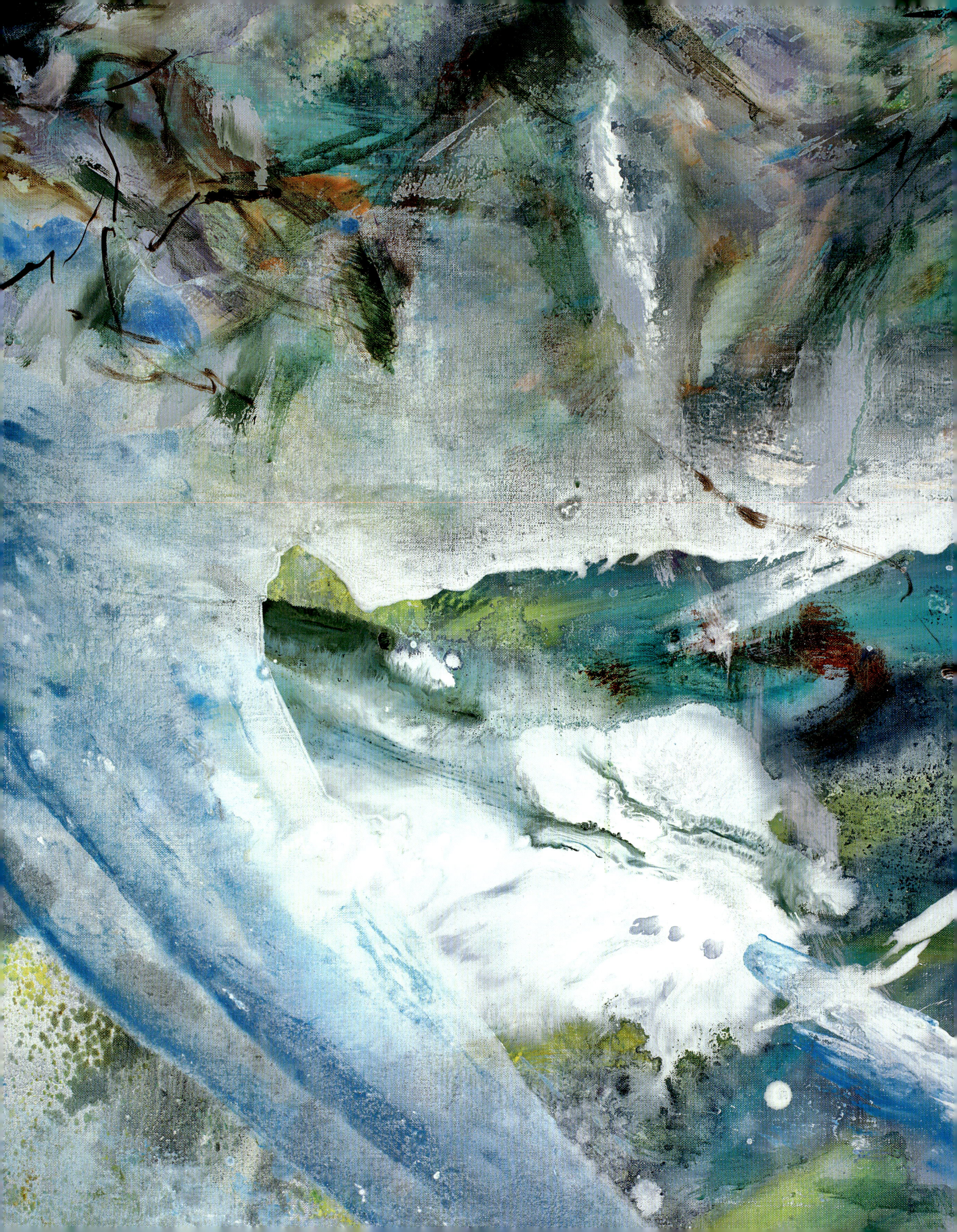

Little Wild Bouquet
2023
oil on linen
74 × 96" | 188 × 243.8 cm

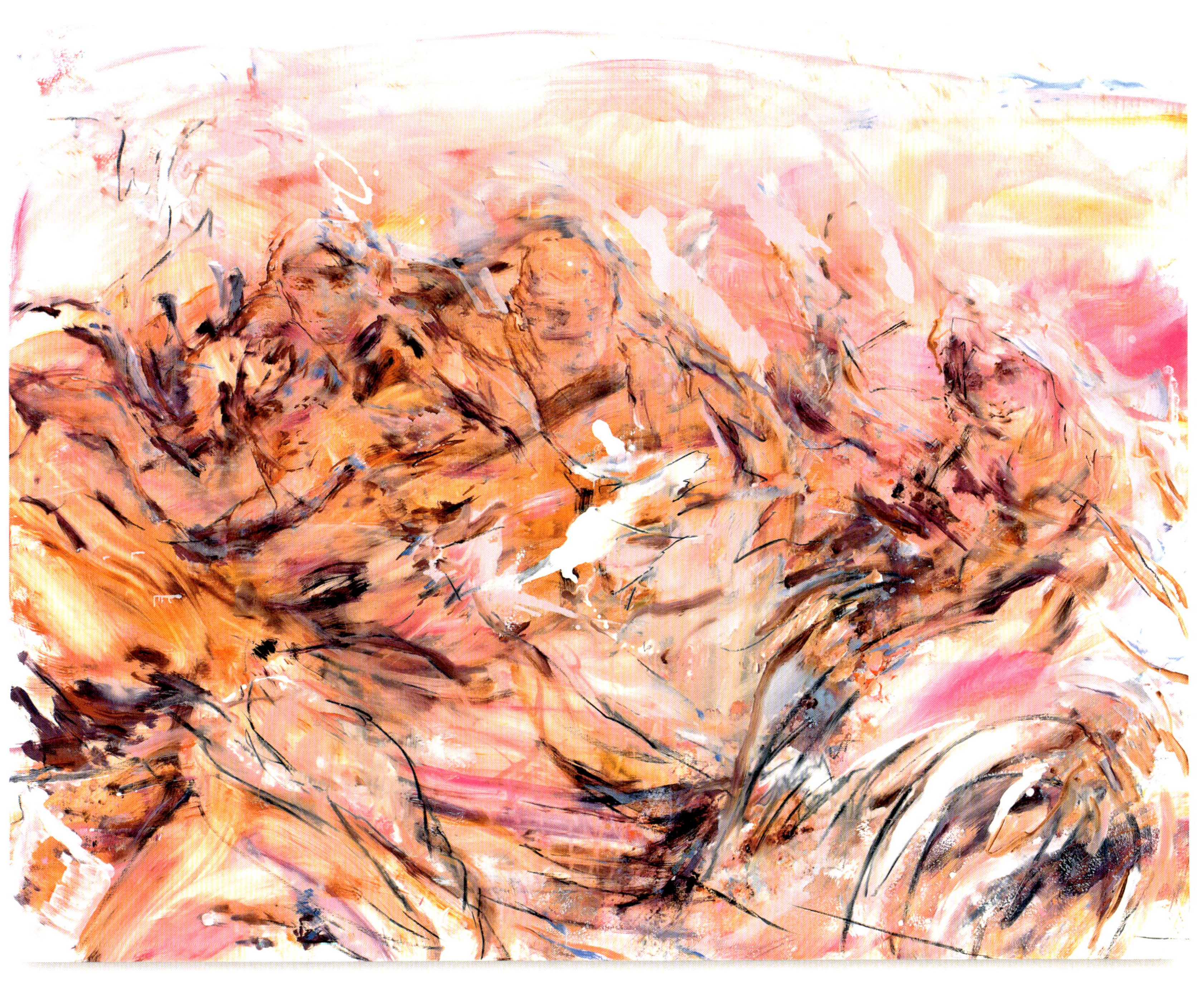

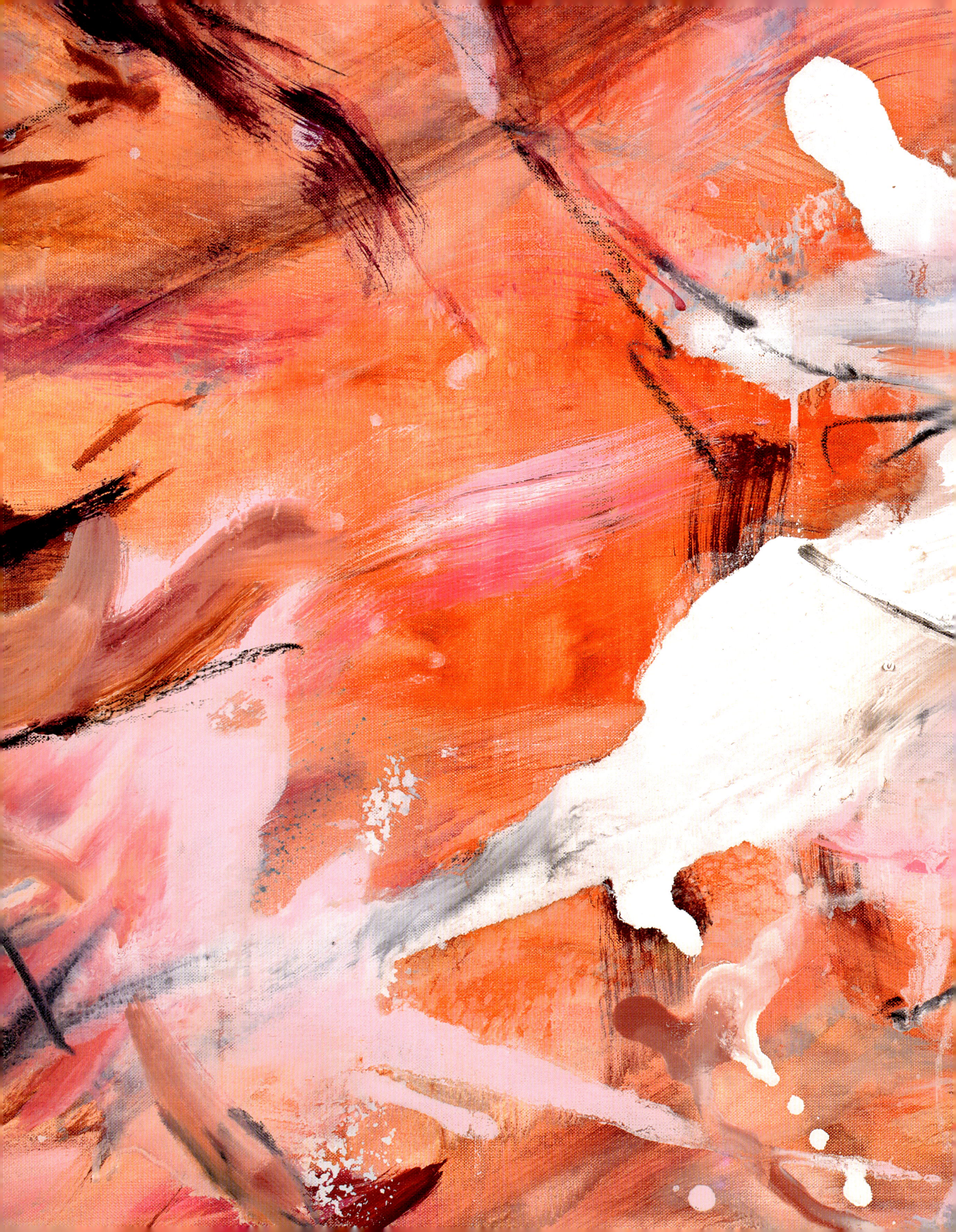

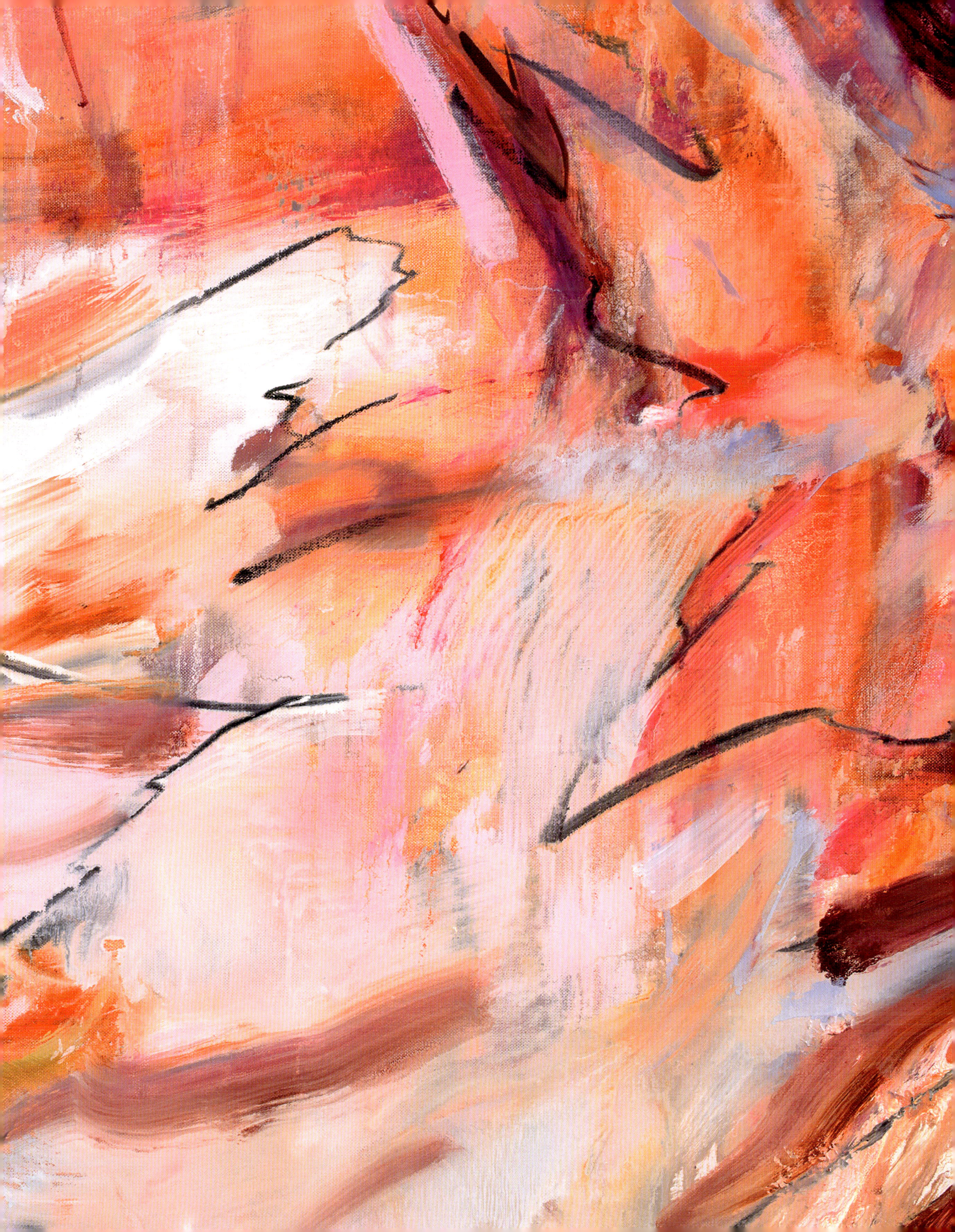

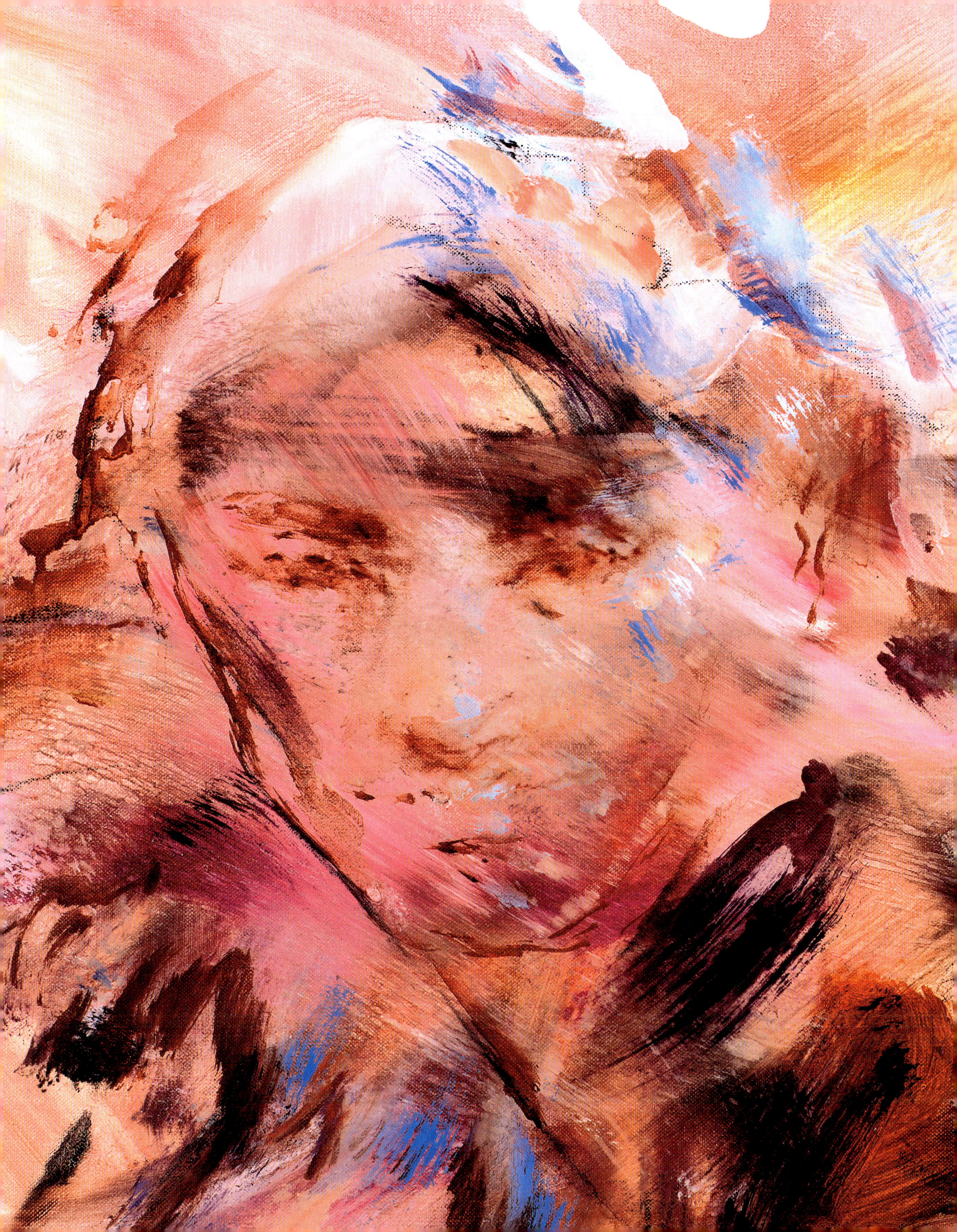

Hippocampus
2023
oil on linen
60 × 80" | 152.4 × 203.2 cm

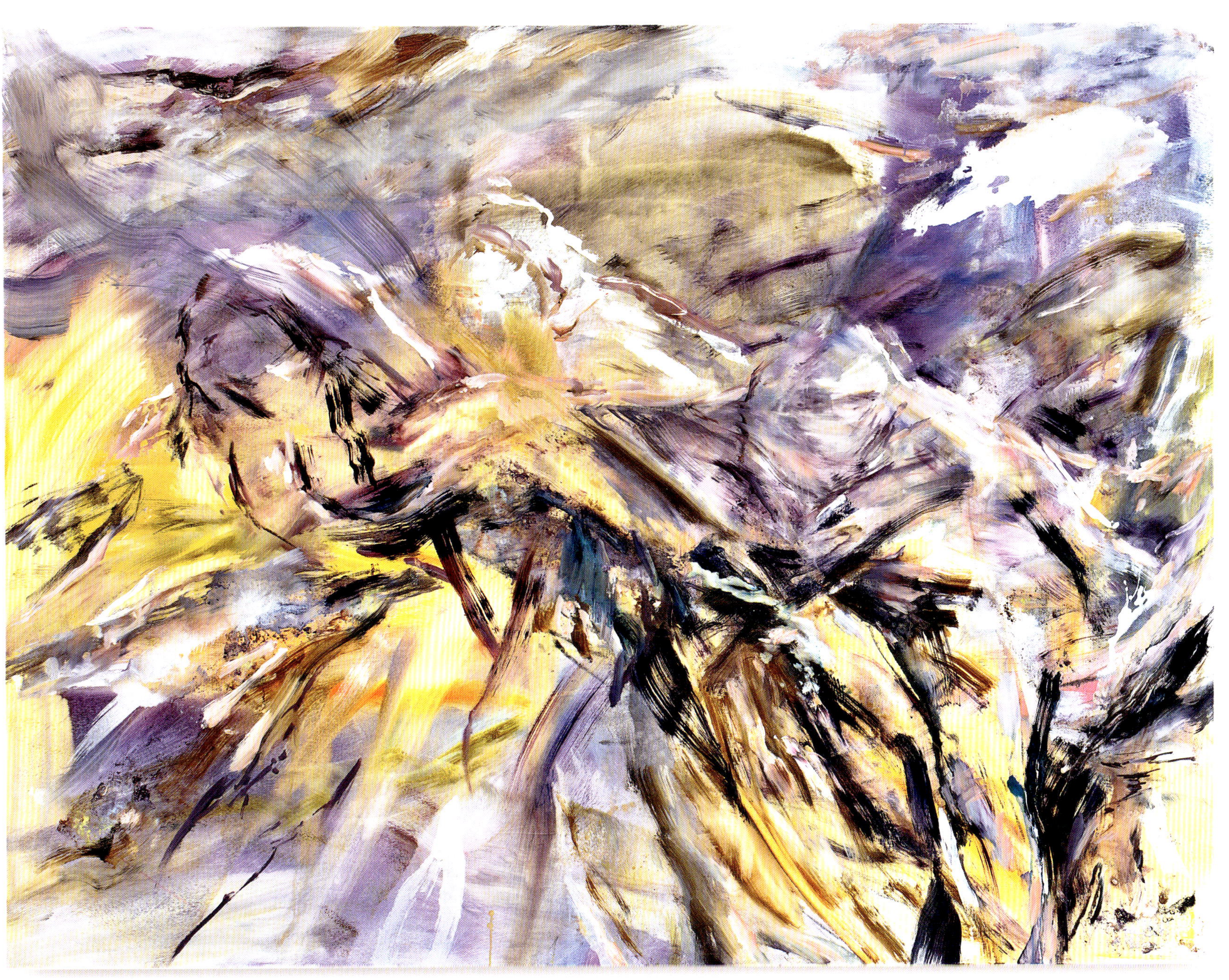

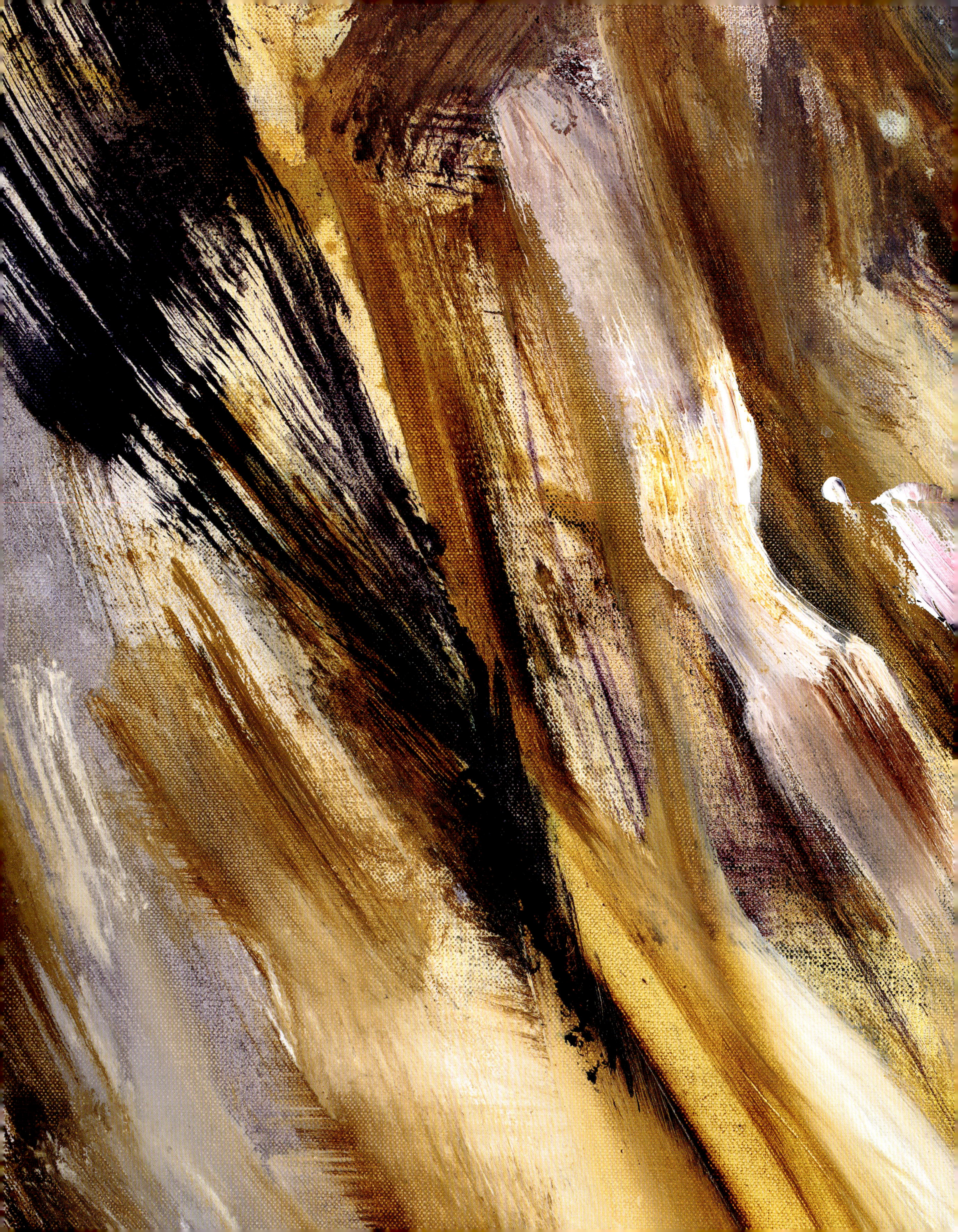

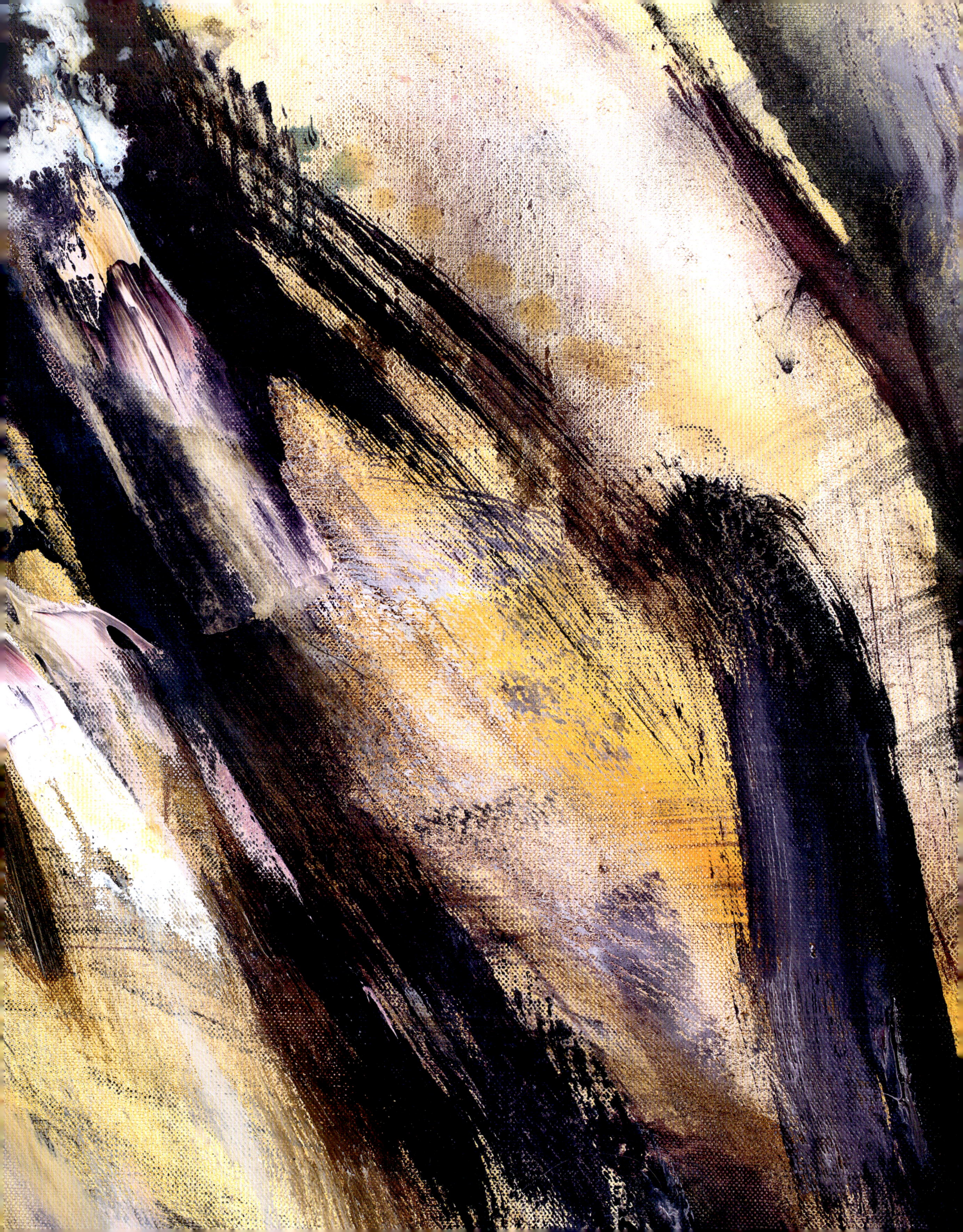

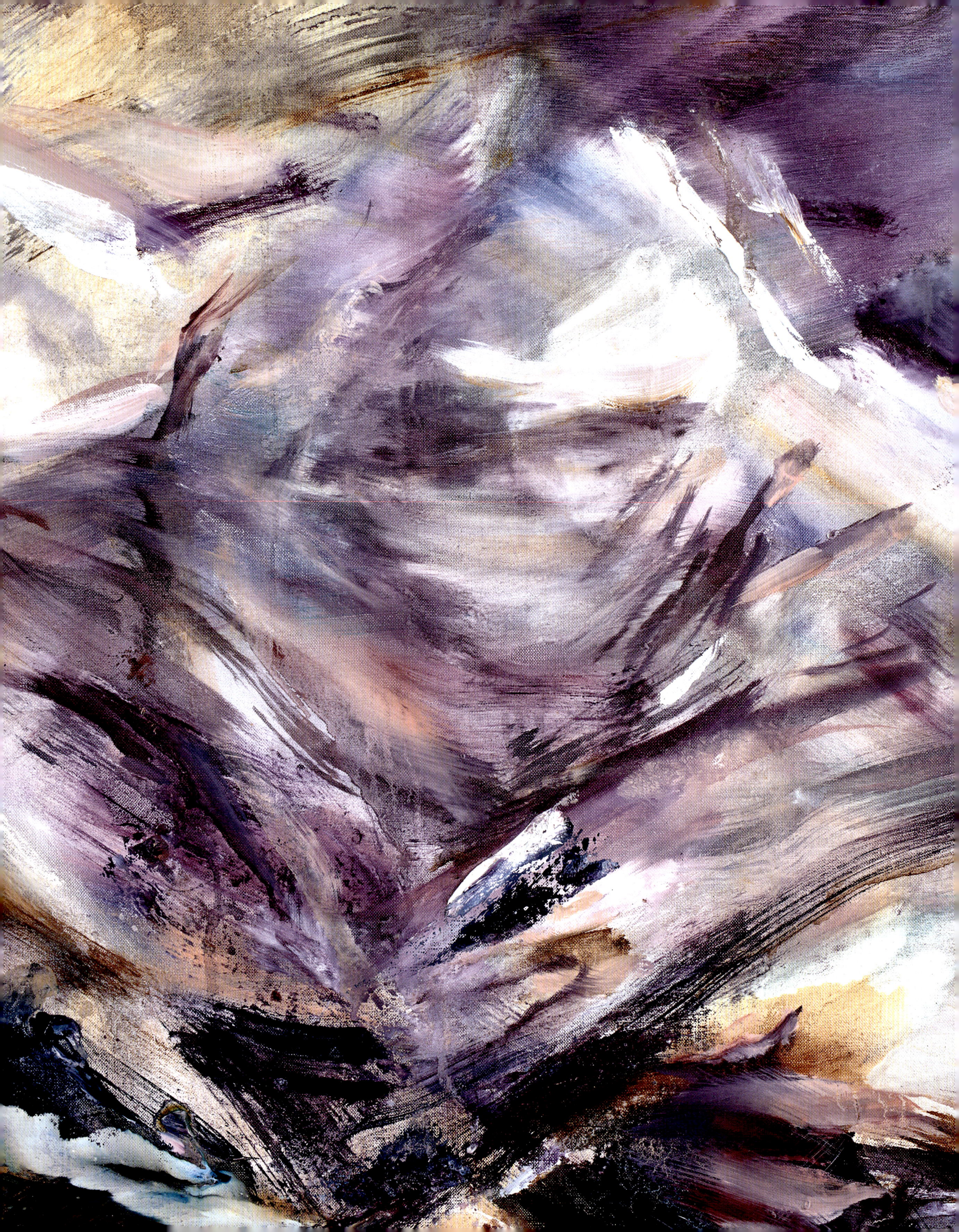

Metronome
2023
oil on linen
80 × 96" | 203.2 × 243.8 cm

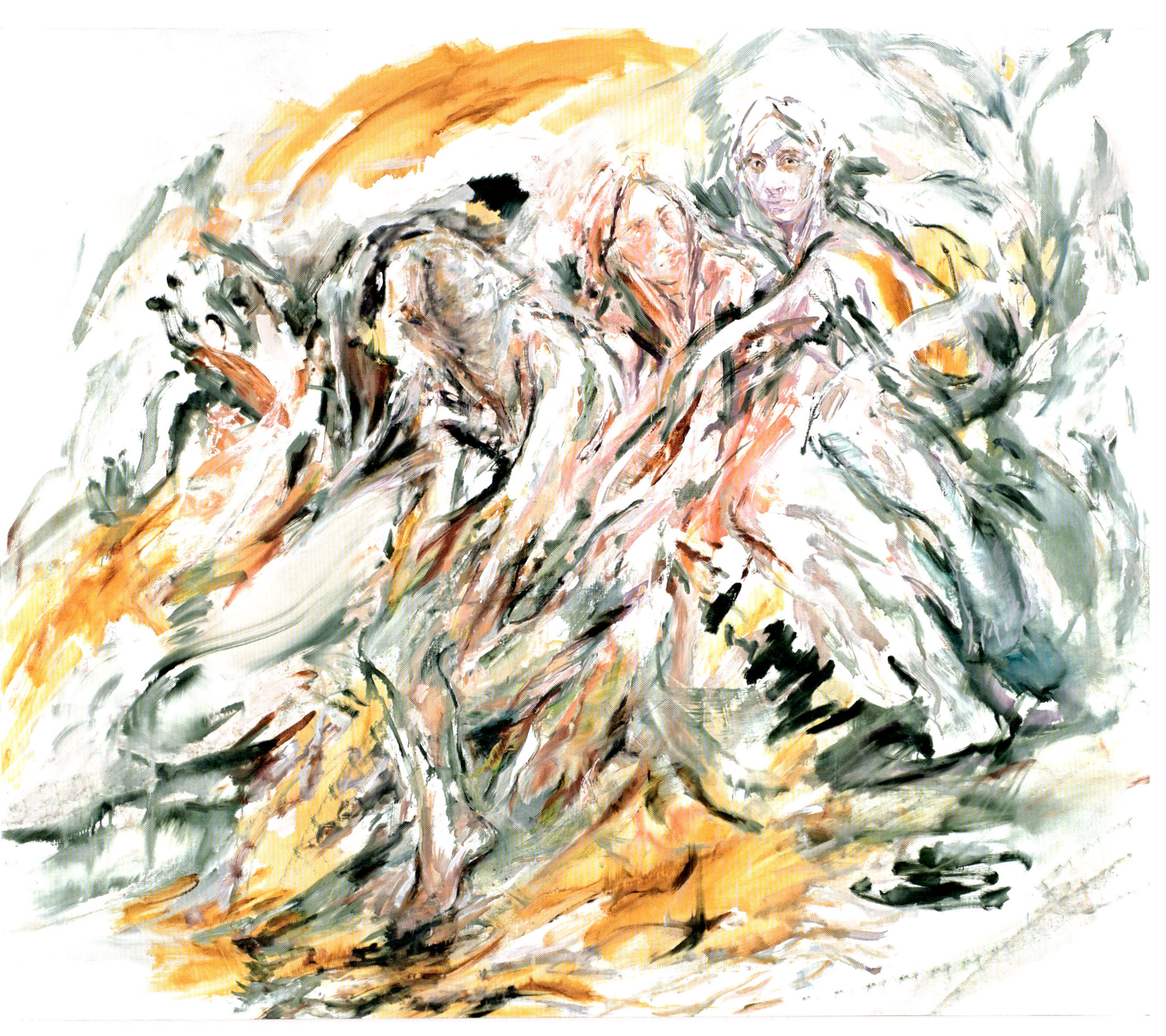

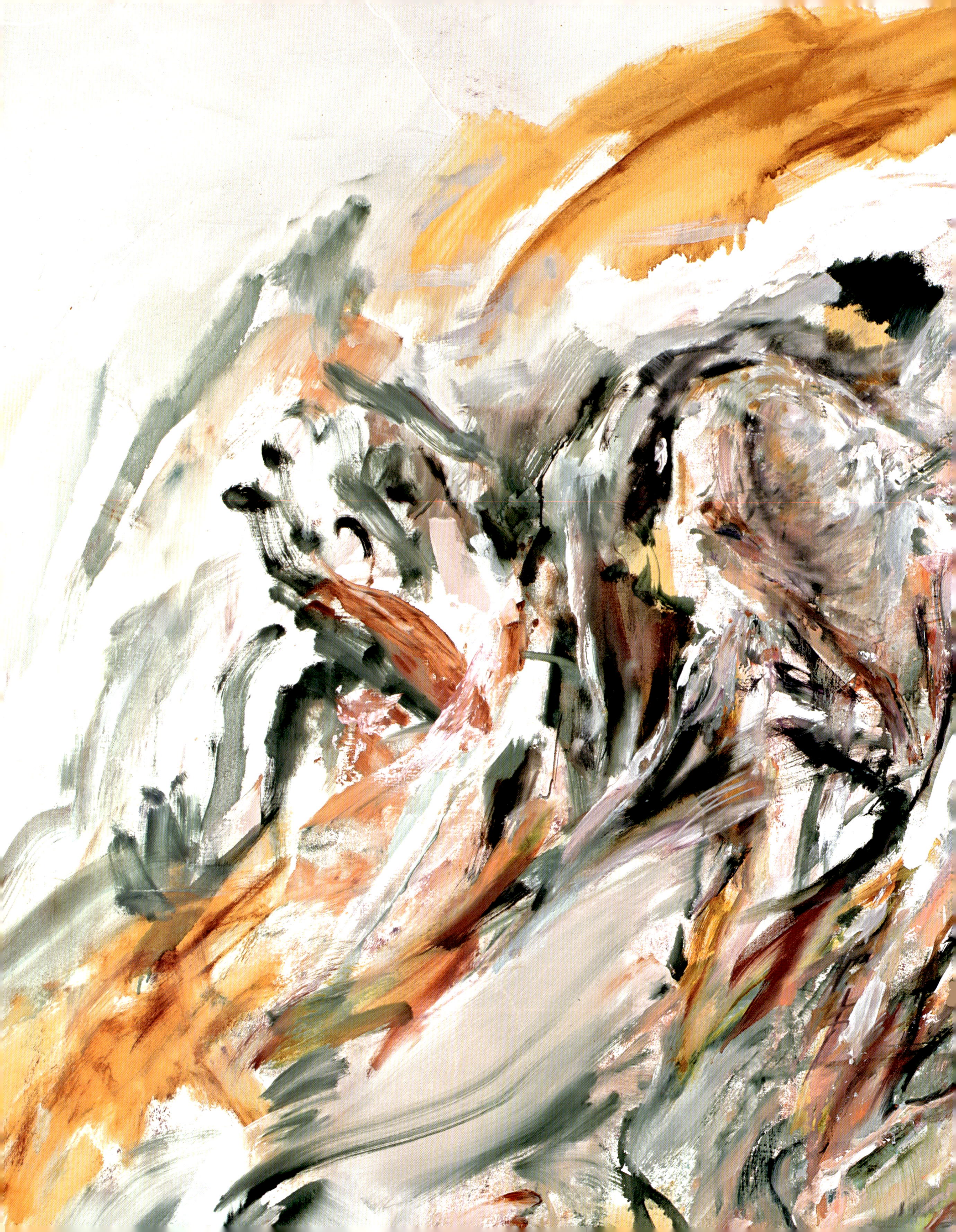

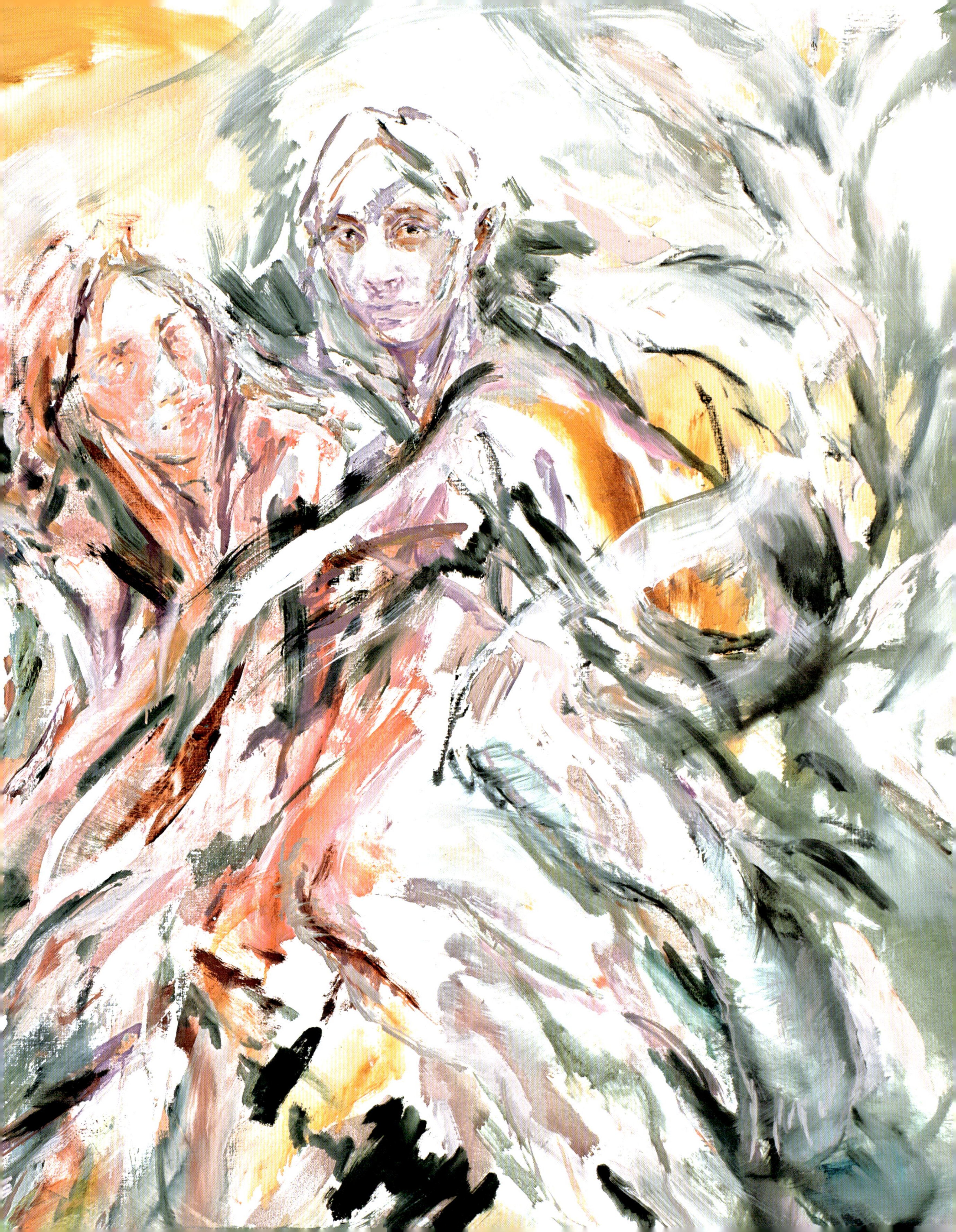

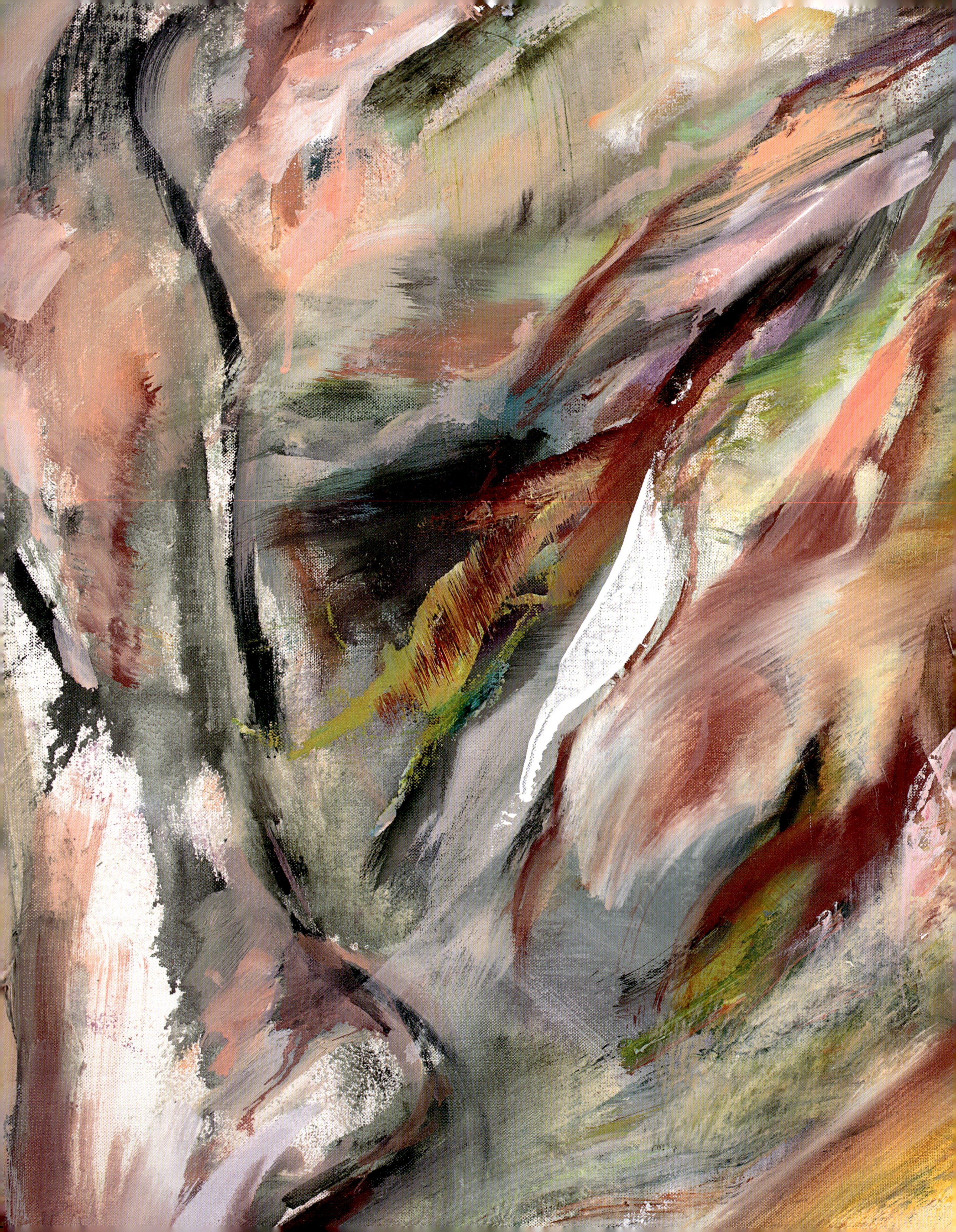

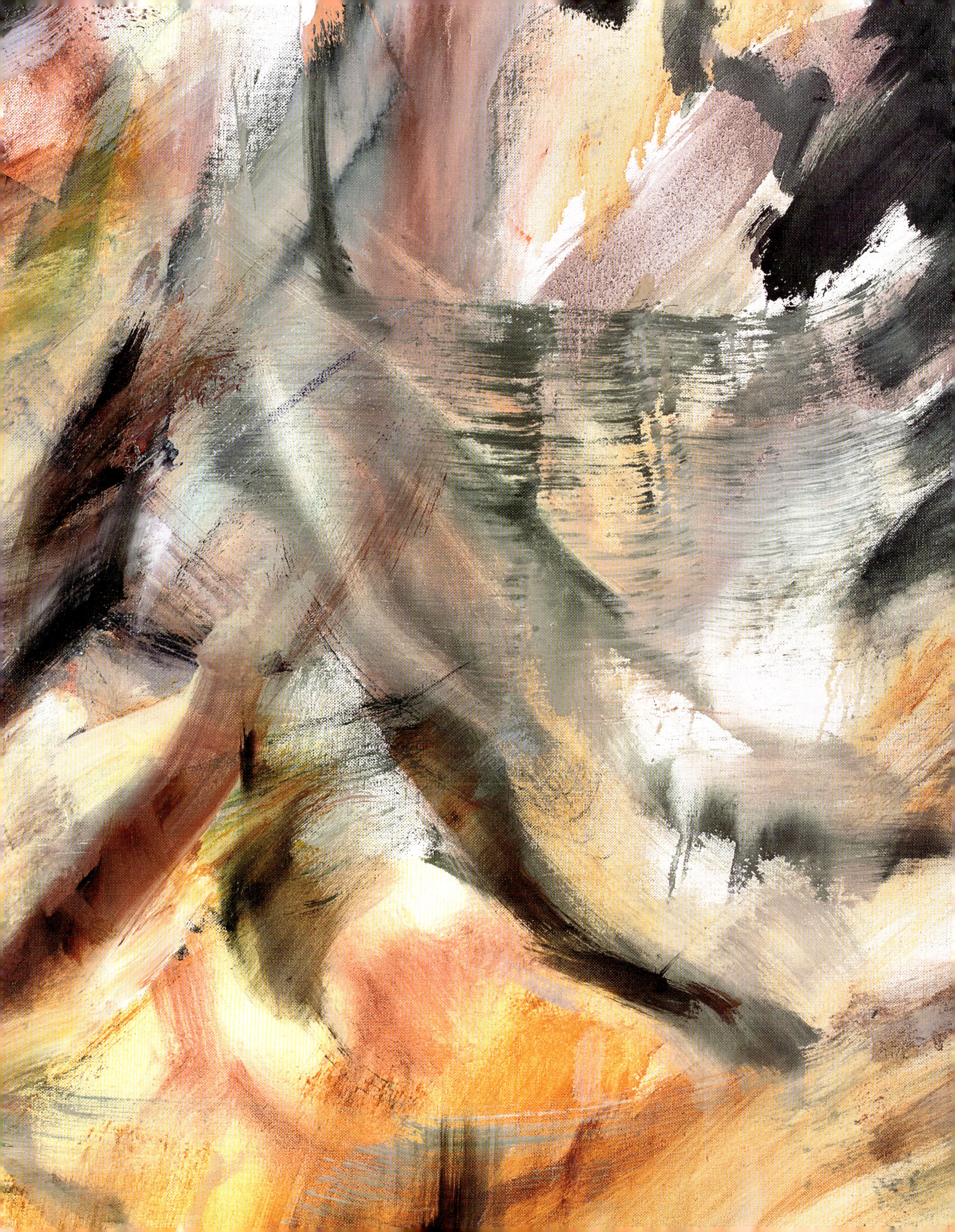

We met when we were almost young
2022
oil on linen
68¼ × 90¼" | 173.4 × 229.2 cm

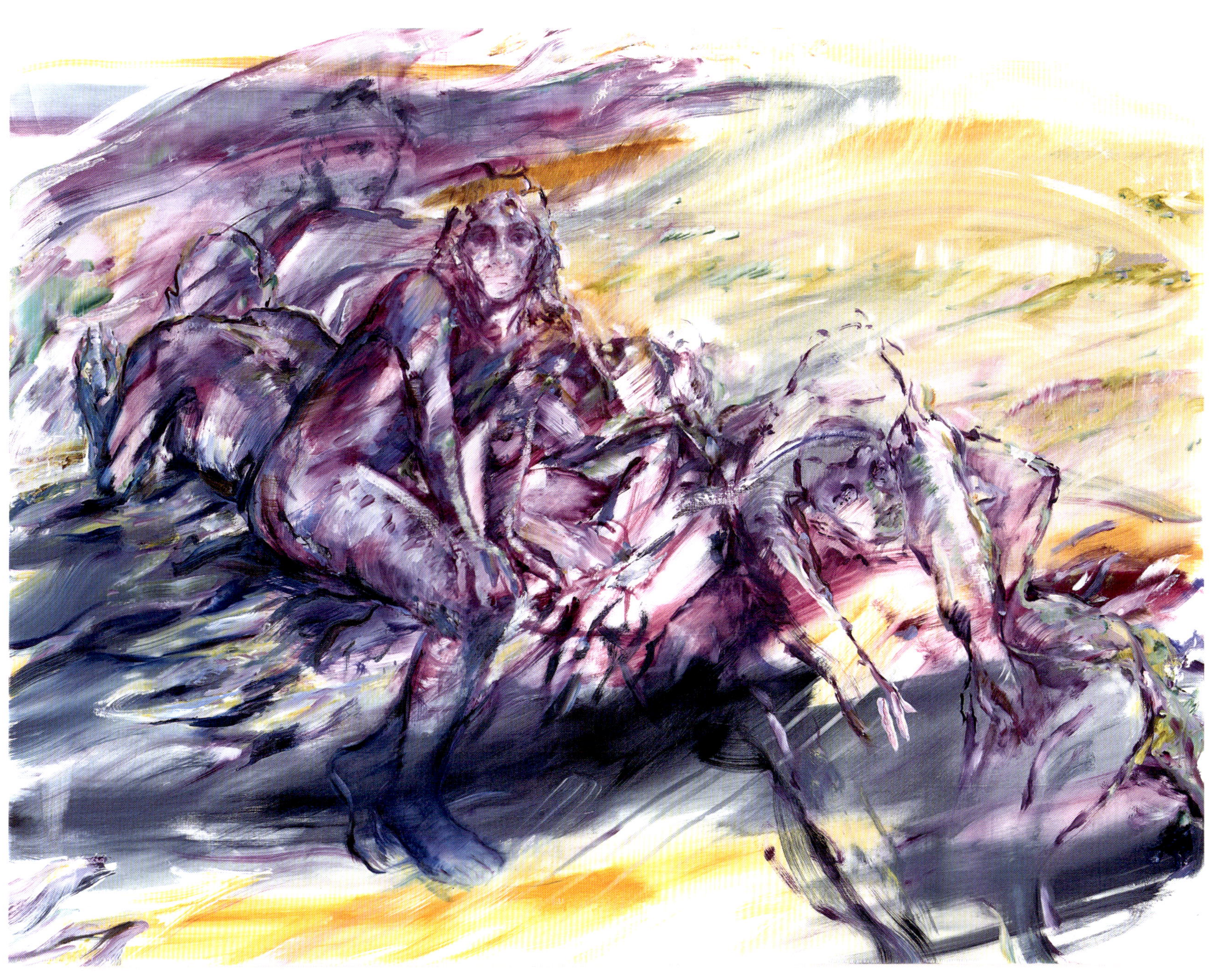

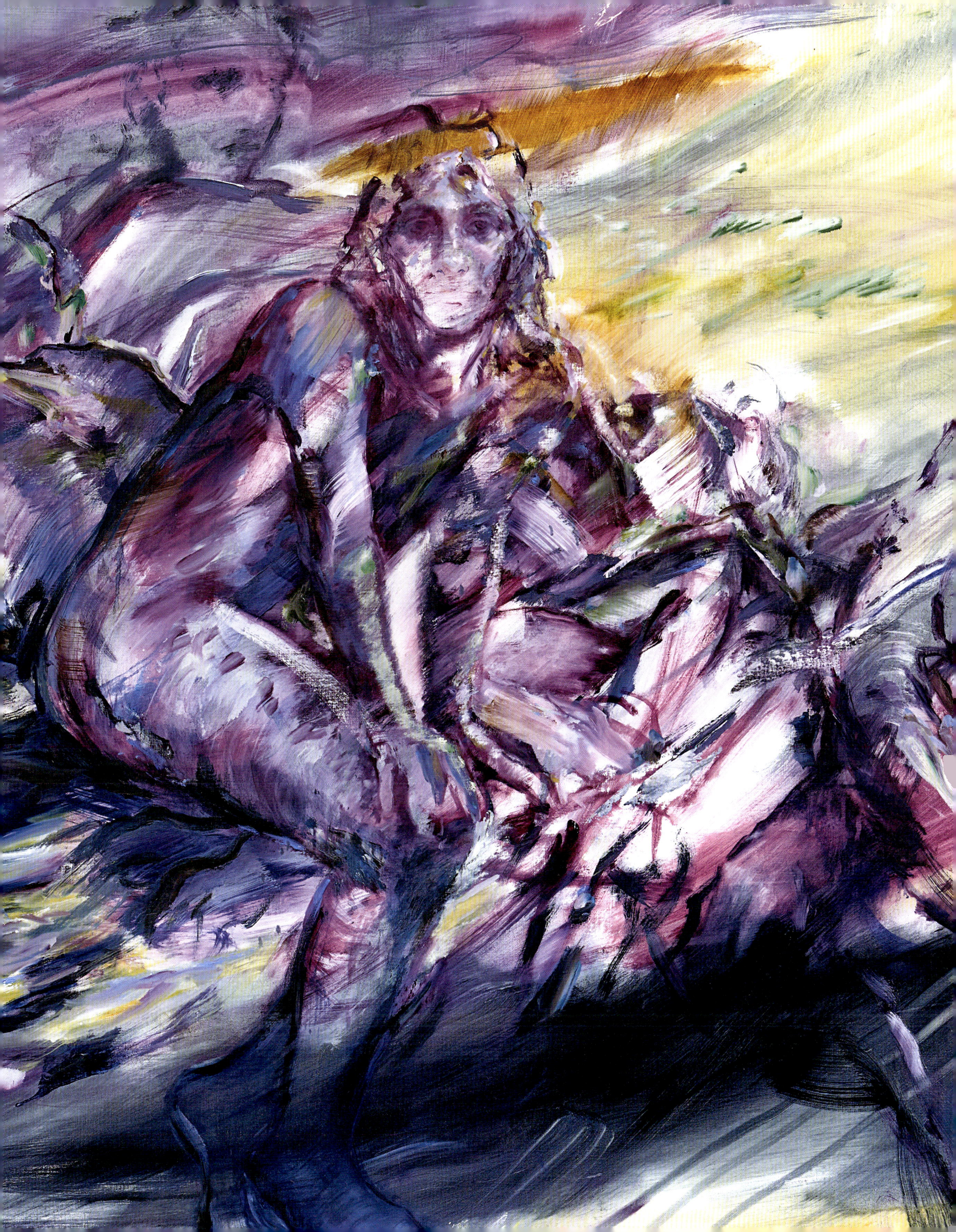

Sea Change
2023
oil on linen
2 panels, 74 × 96" | 188 × 243.8 cm each
148 × 96" | 375.9 × 243.8 cm overall

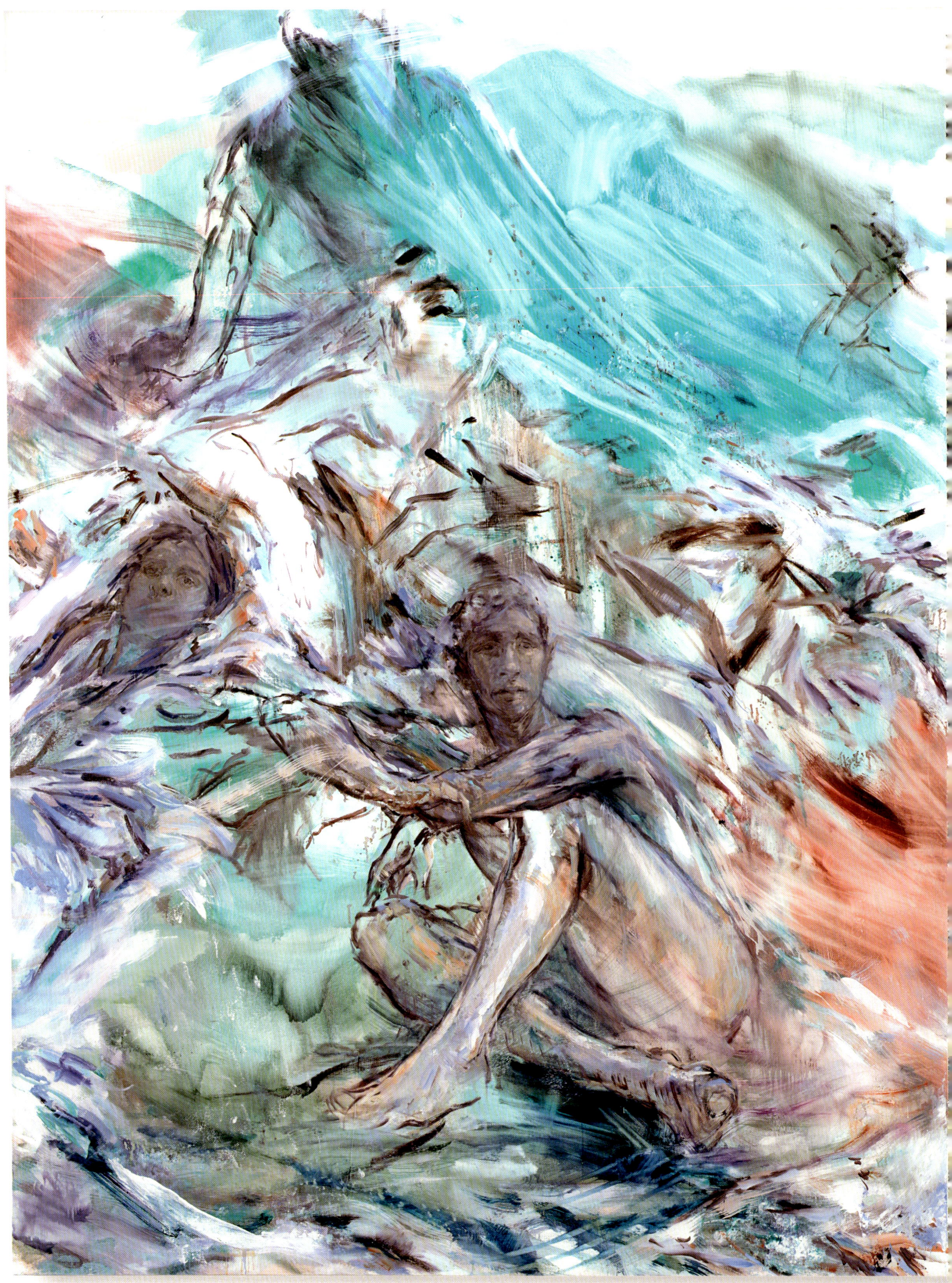

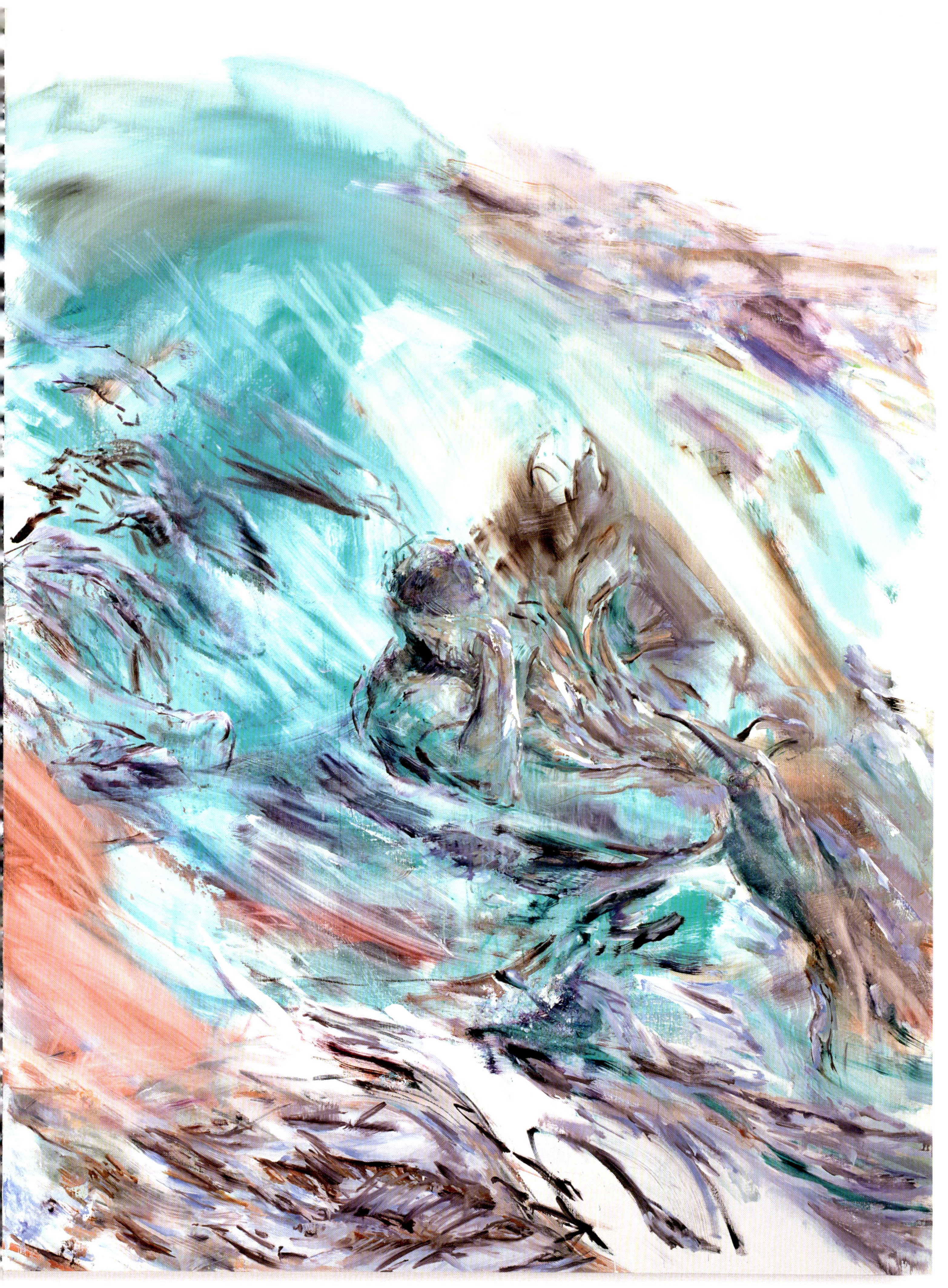

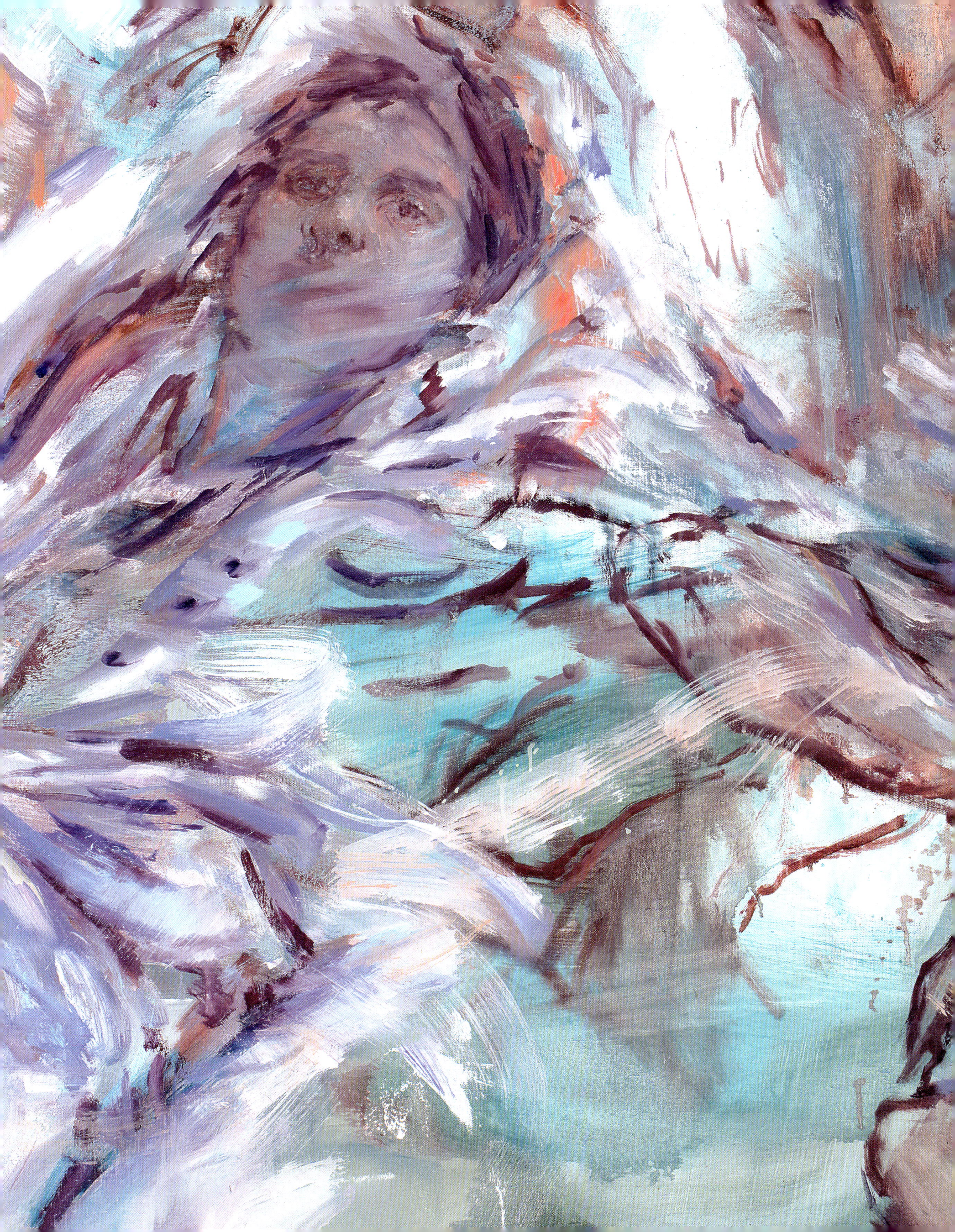

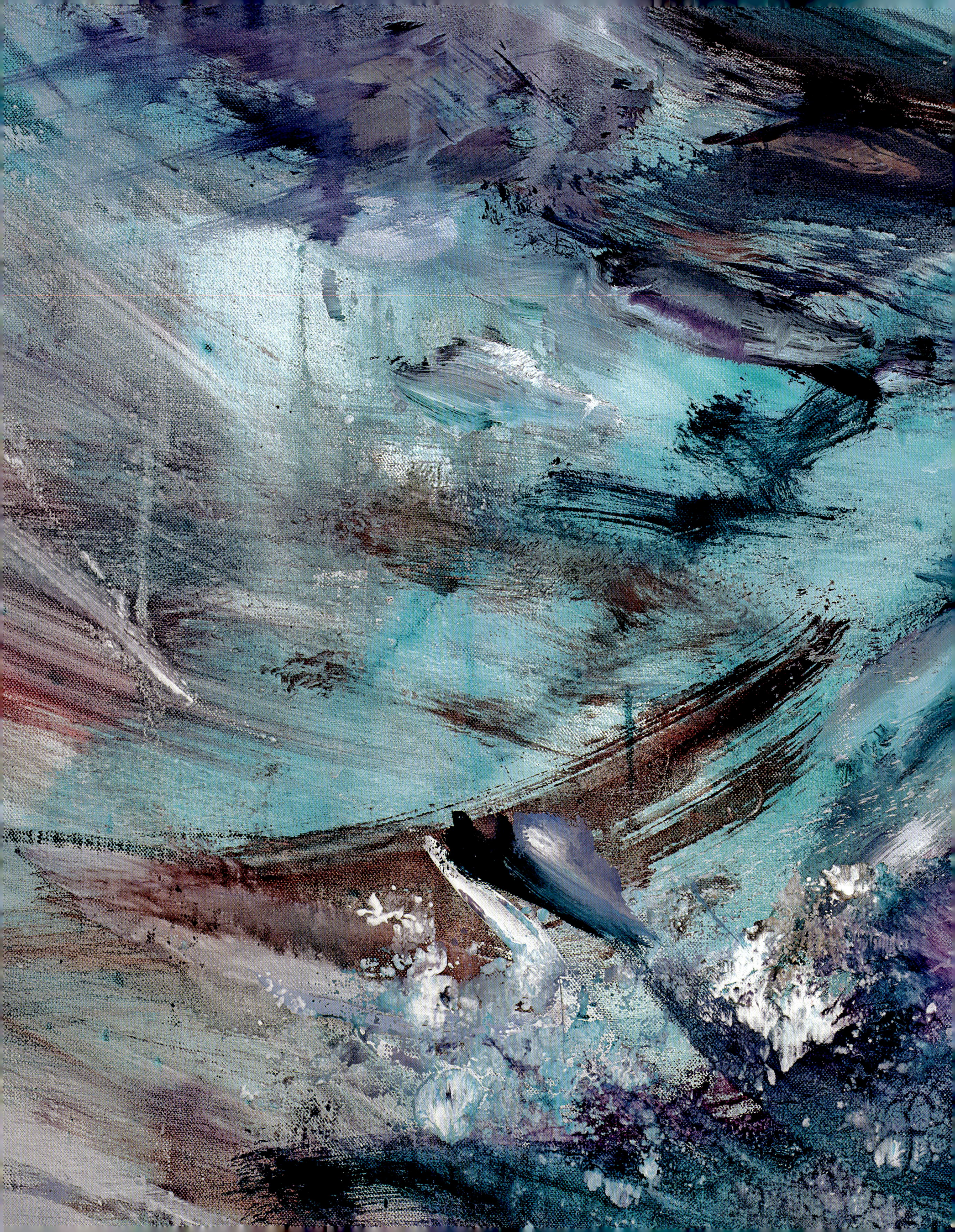

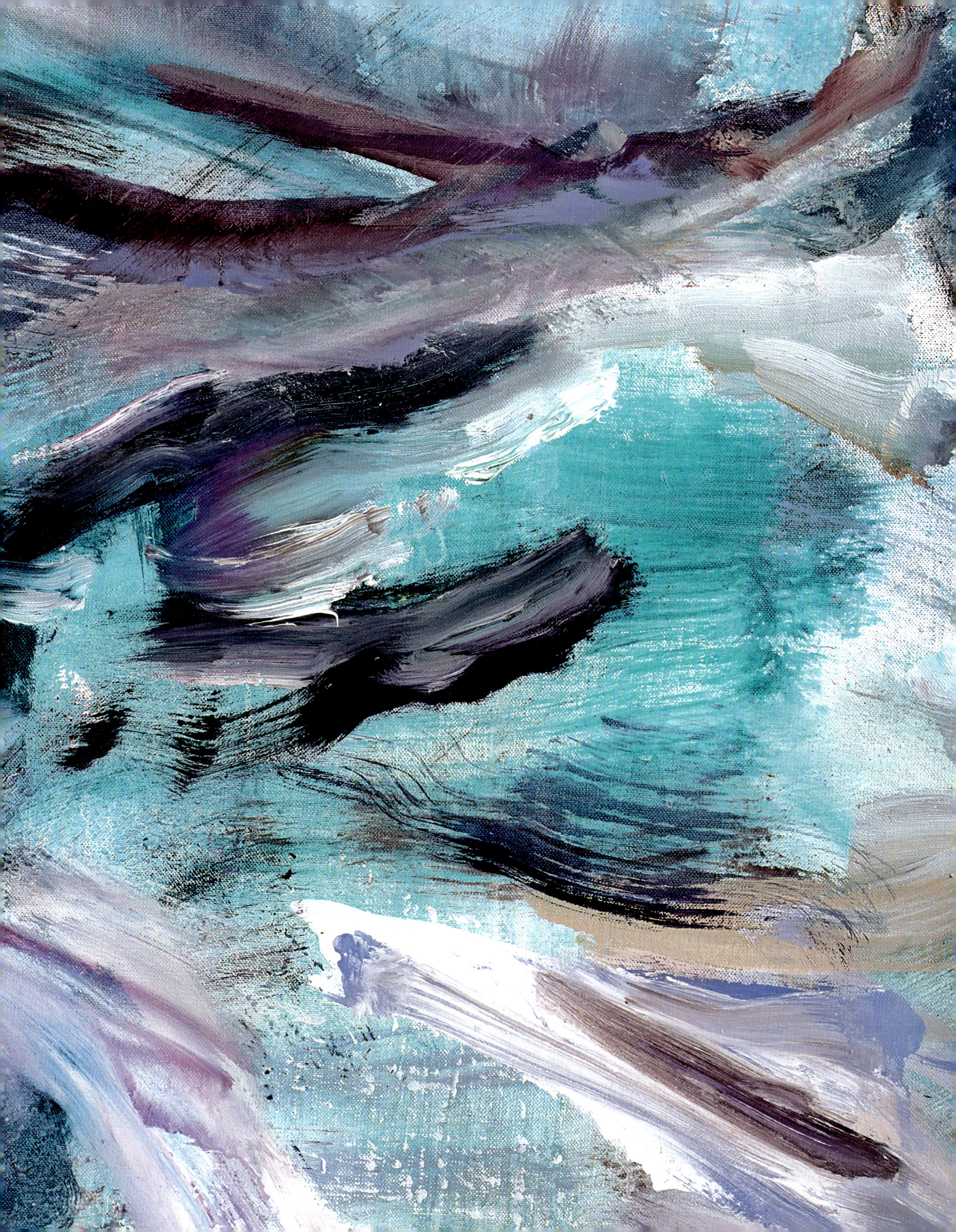

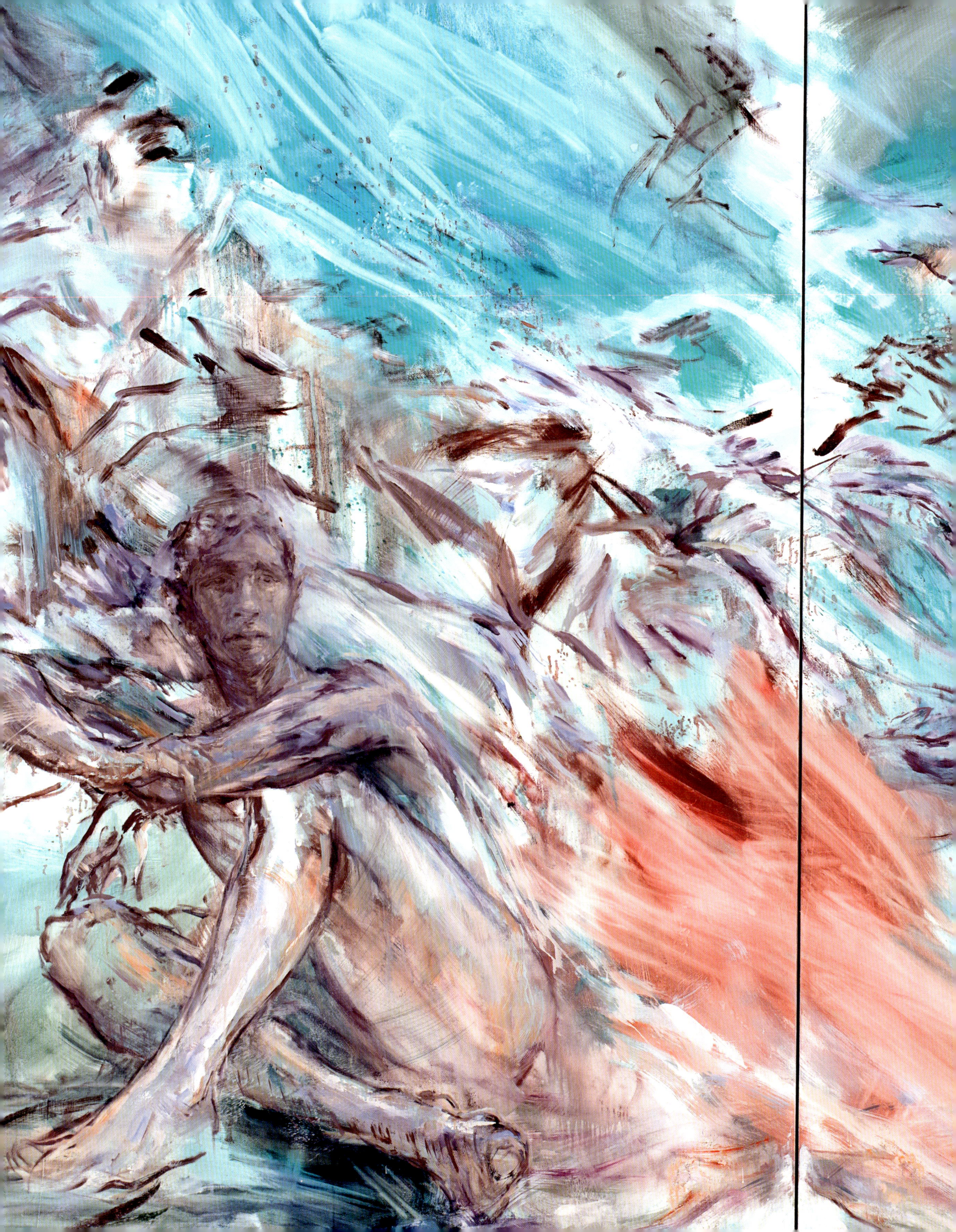

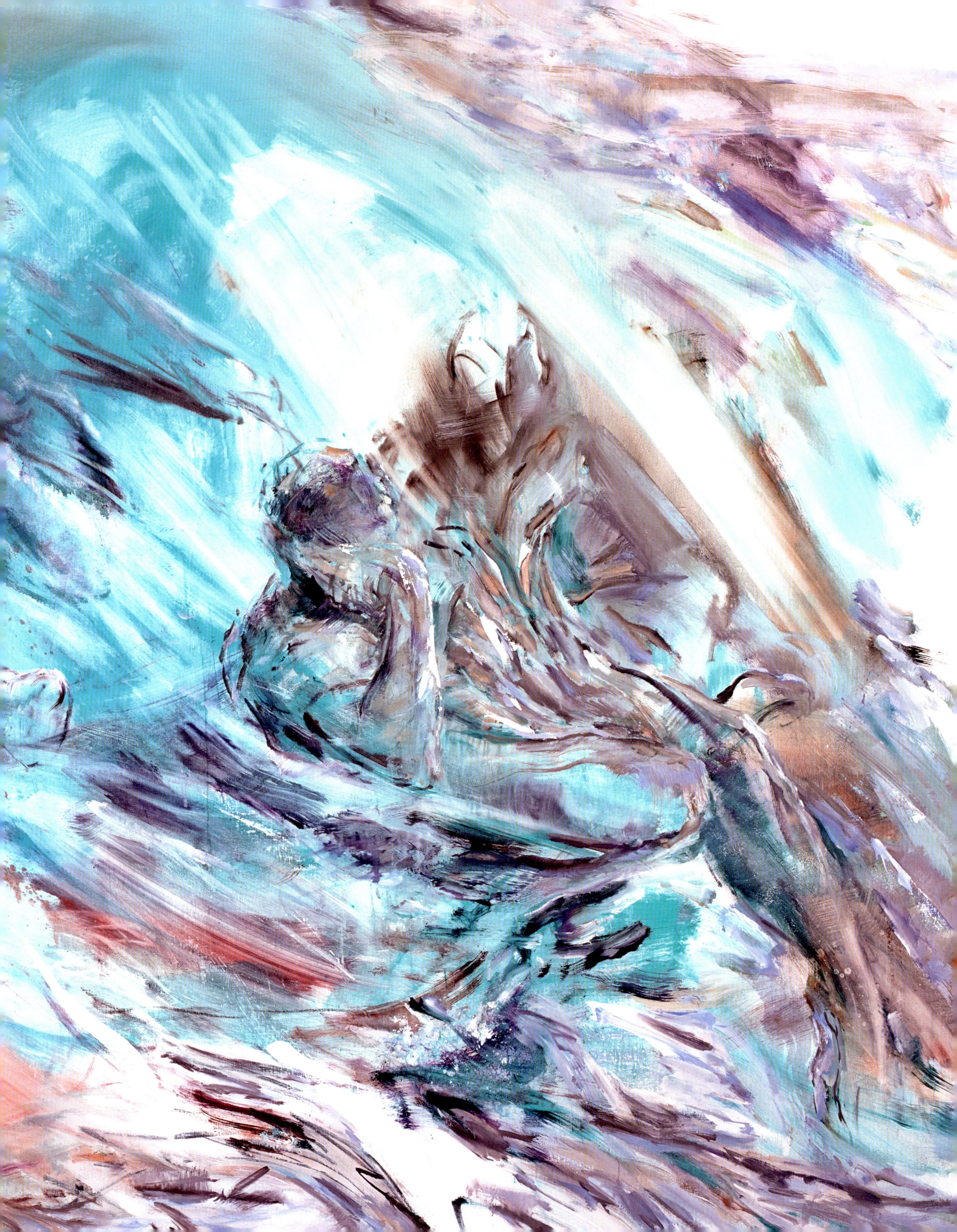

Montserrat
2023
oil on linen
60×72" | 152.4×182.9 cm

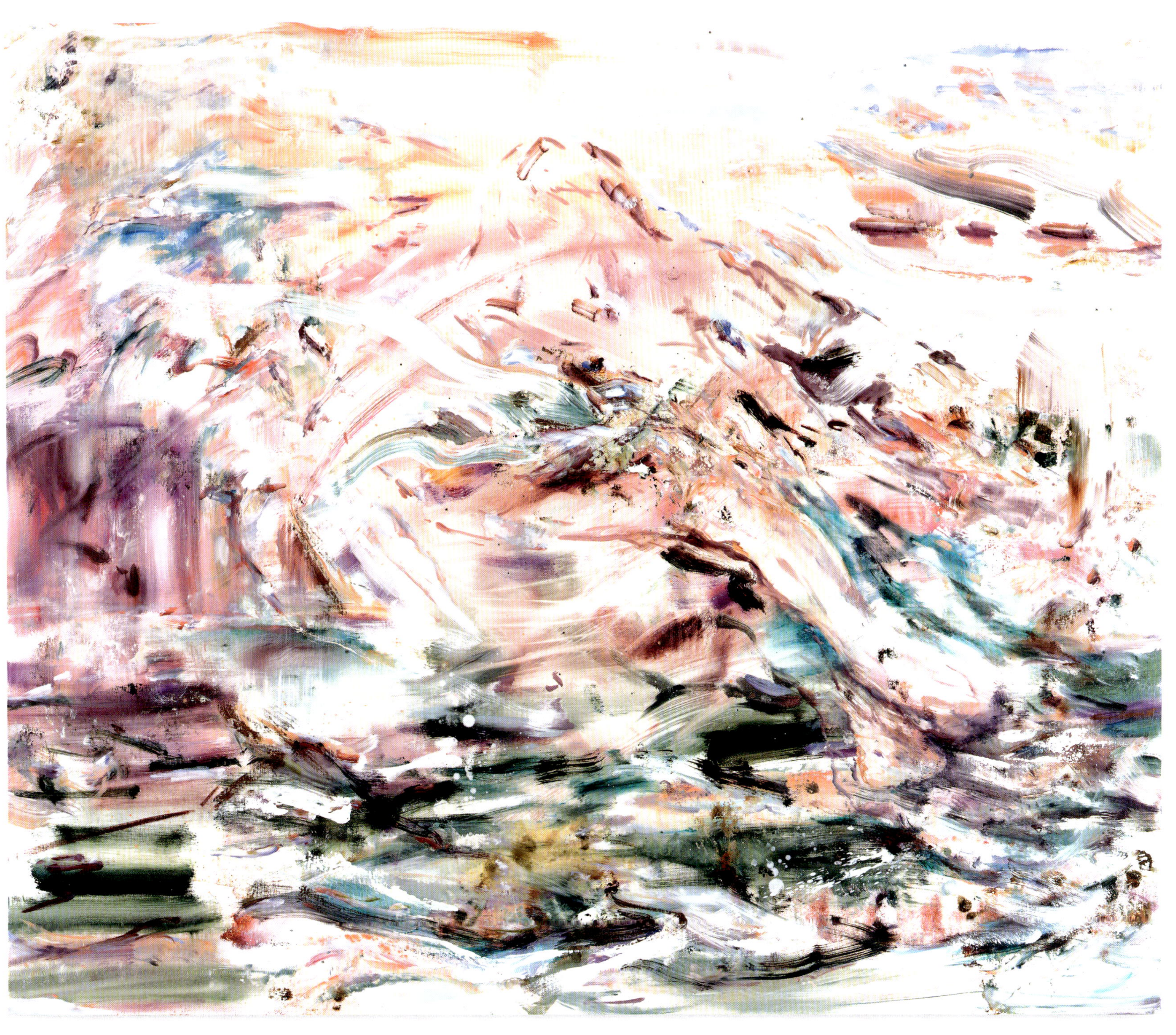

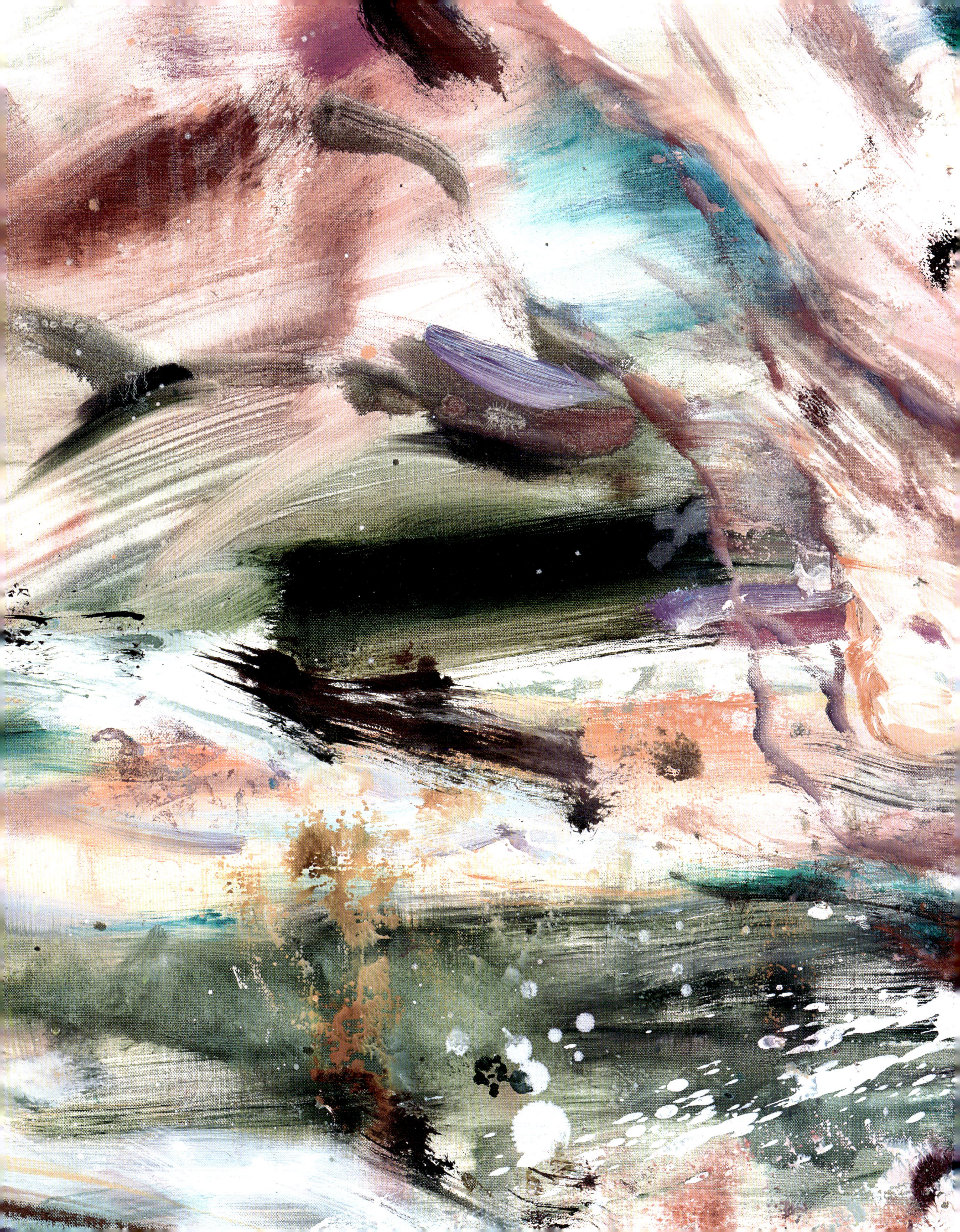

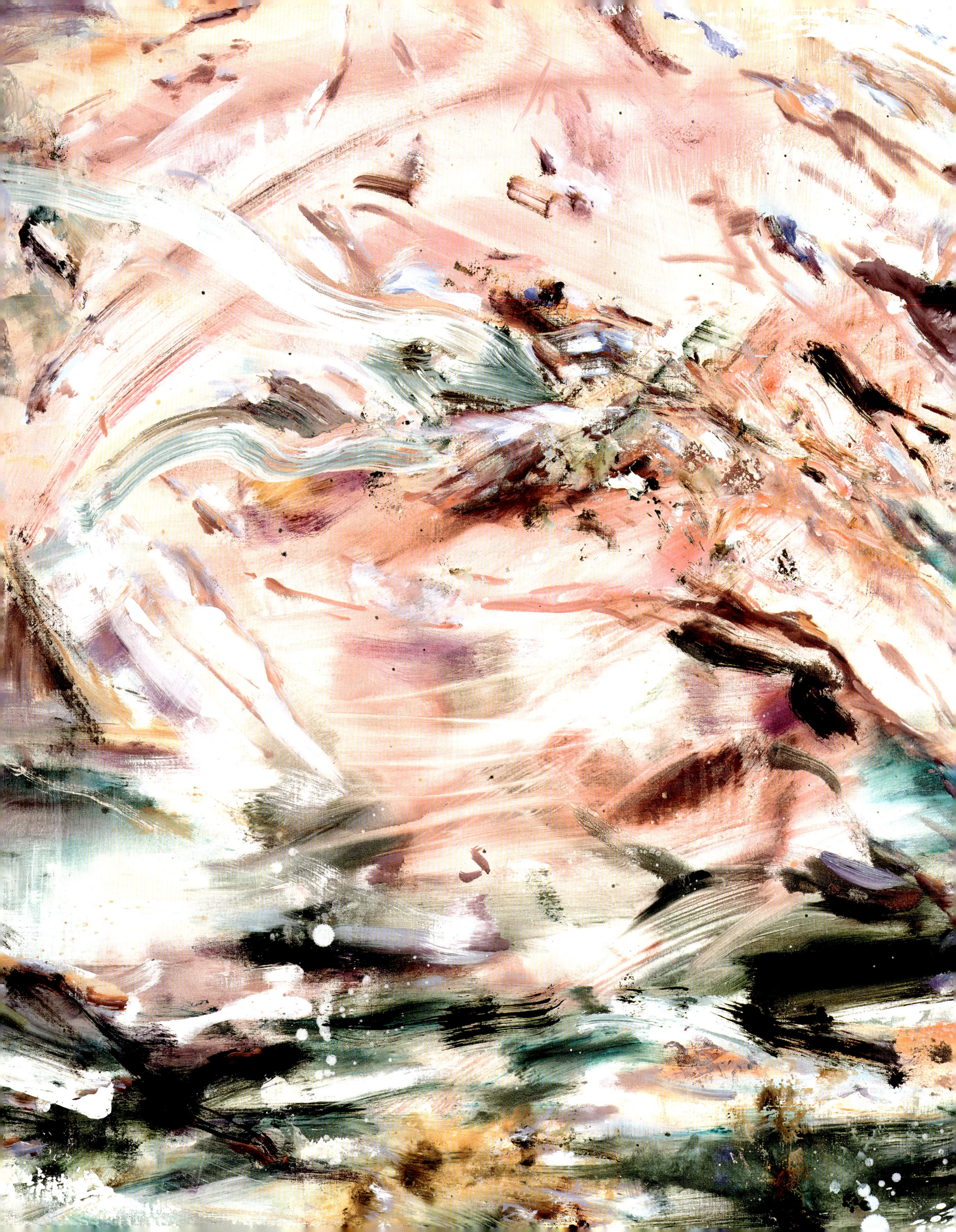

Pareidola
2023
oil on linen
74 × 96" | 188 × 243.8 cm

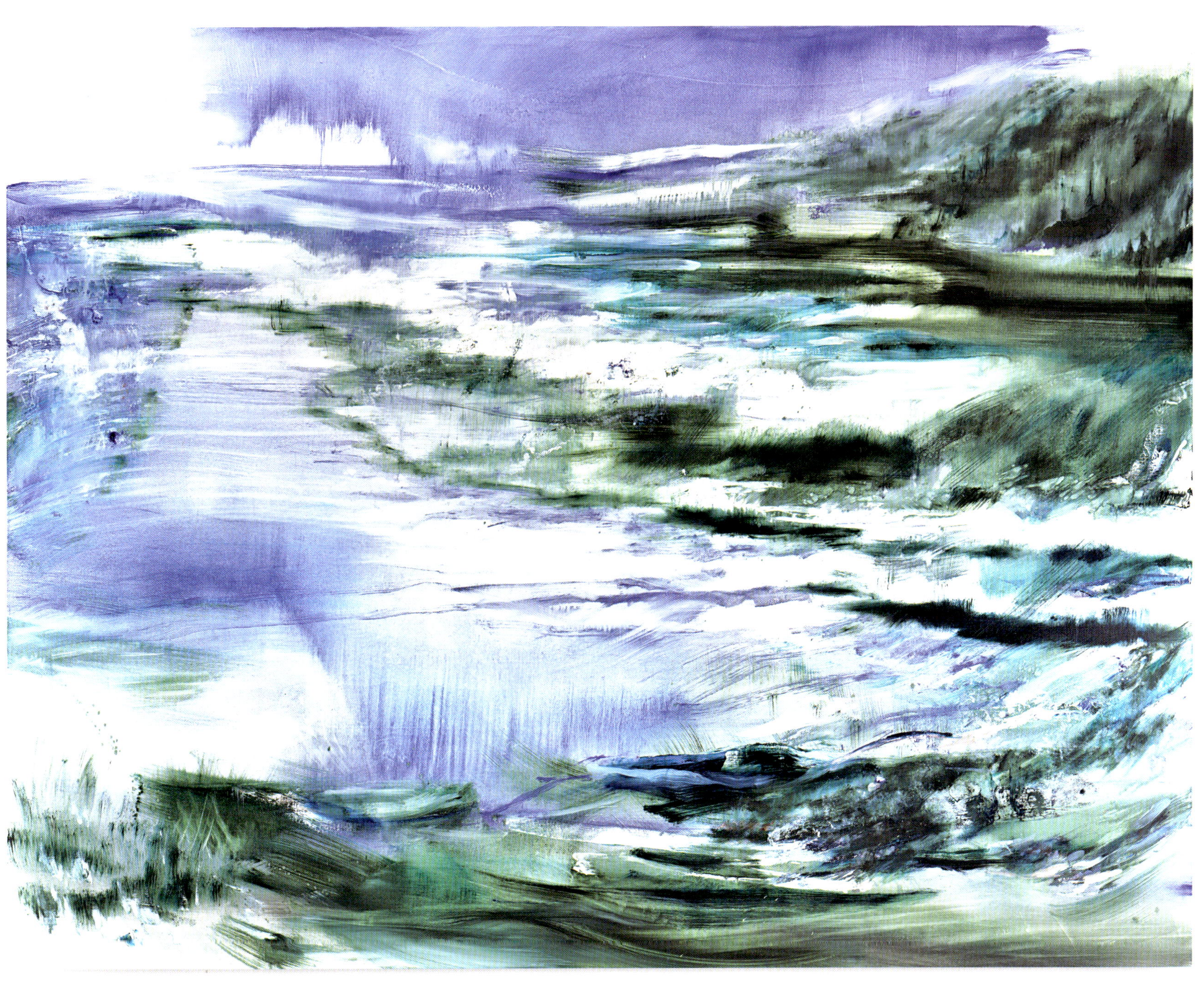

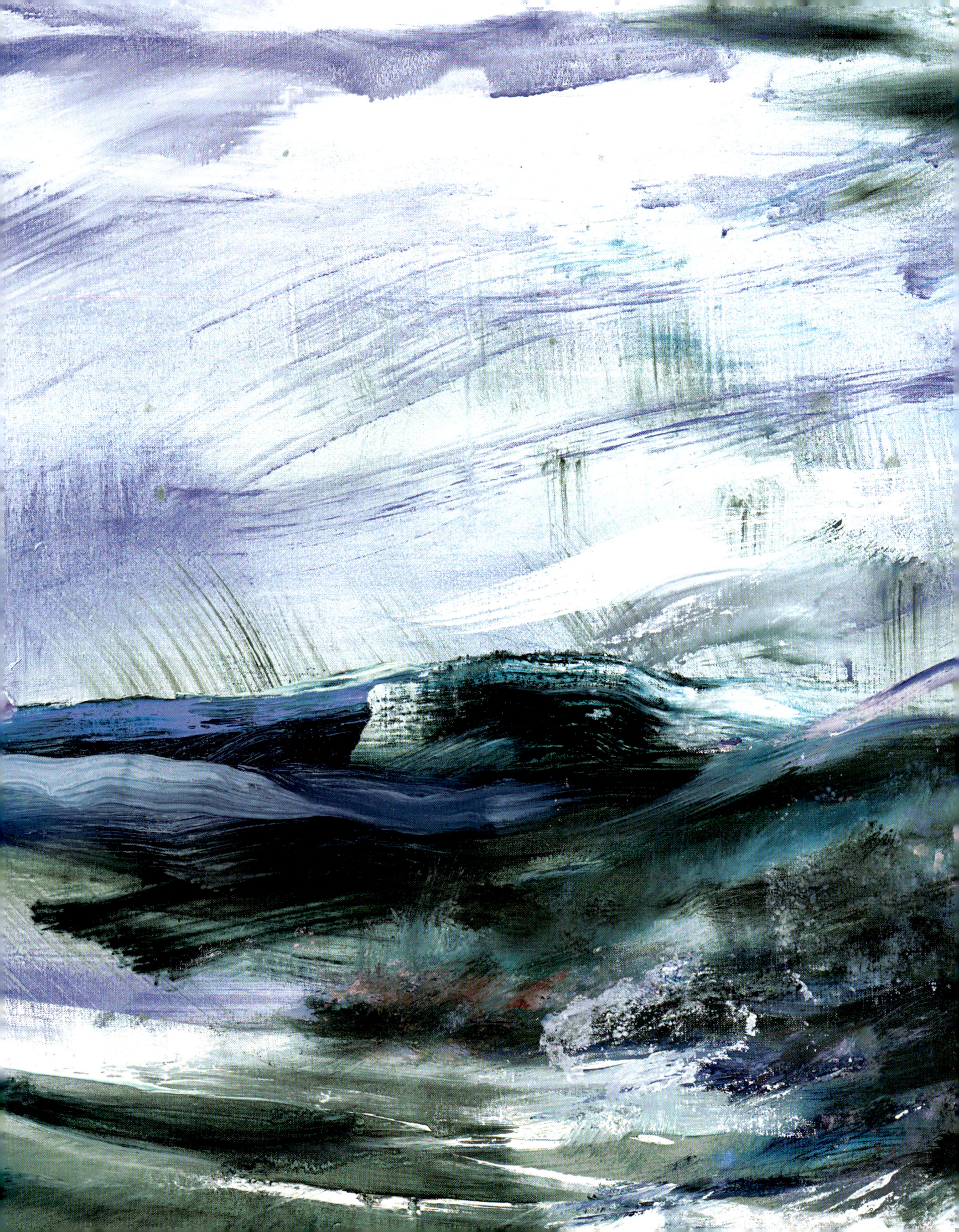

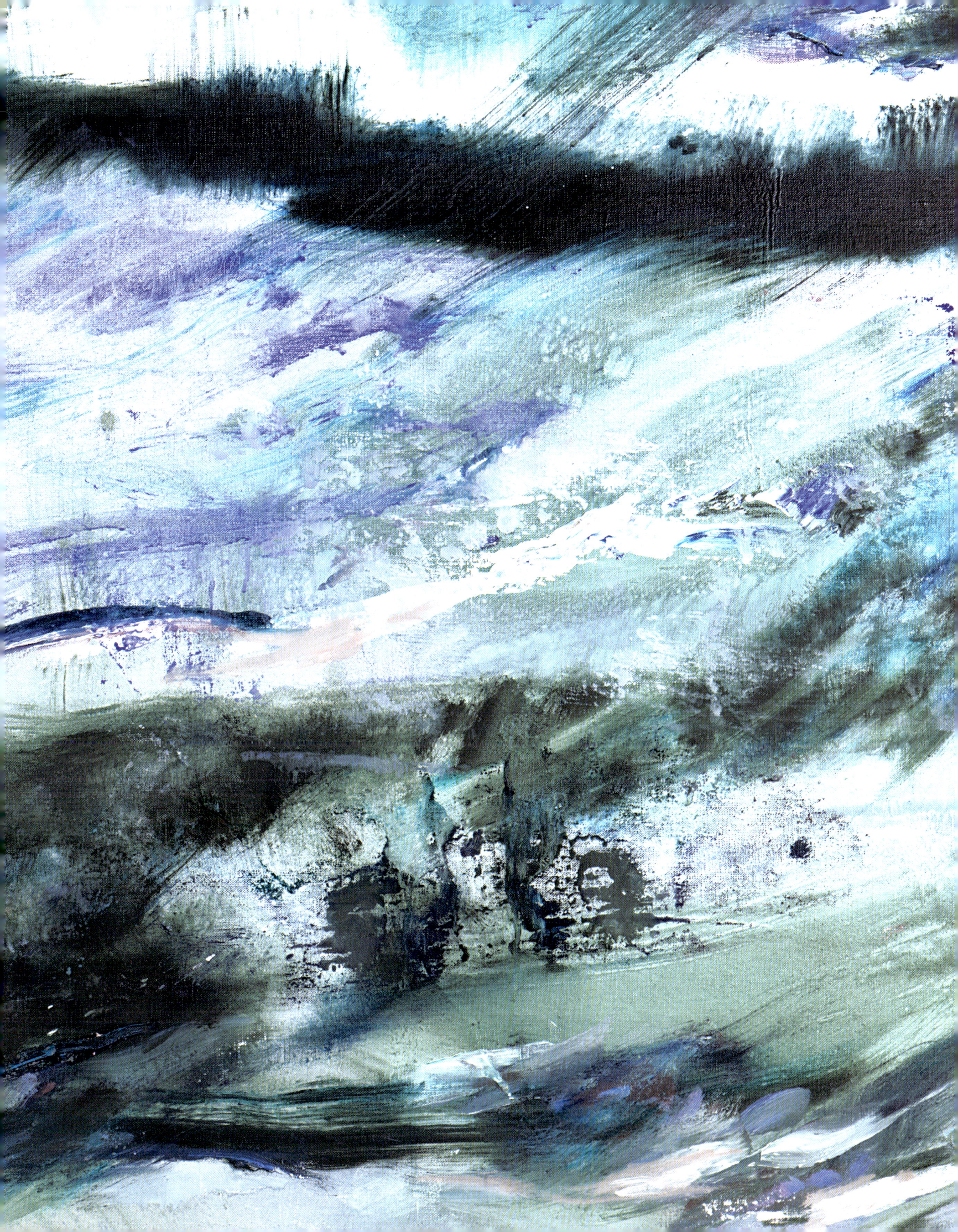

You into me, me into you
2023
oil on linen
74×96" | 188×243.8 cm

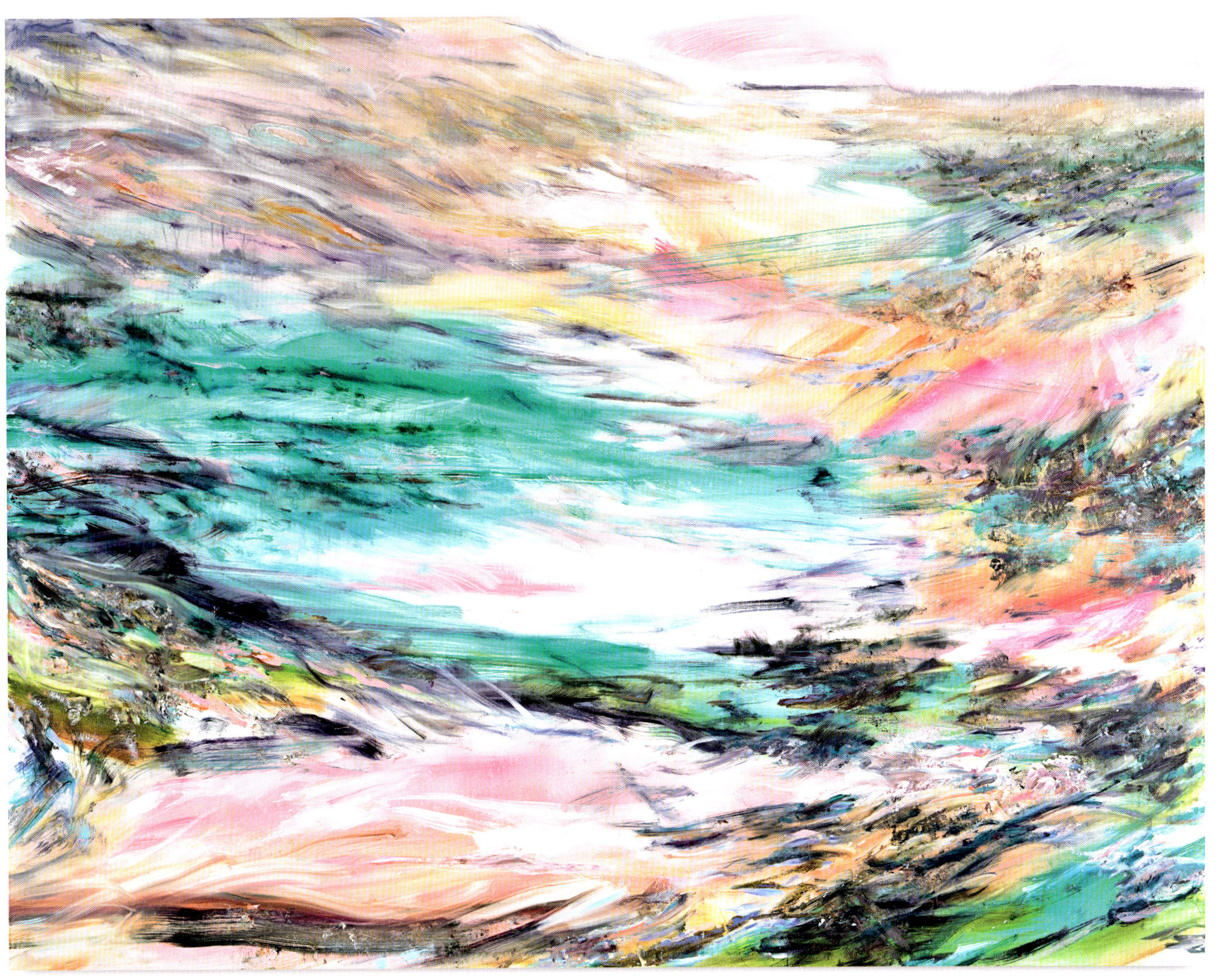

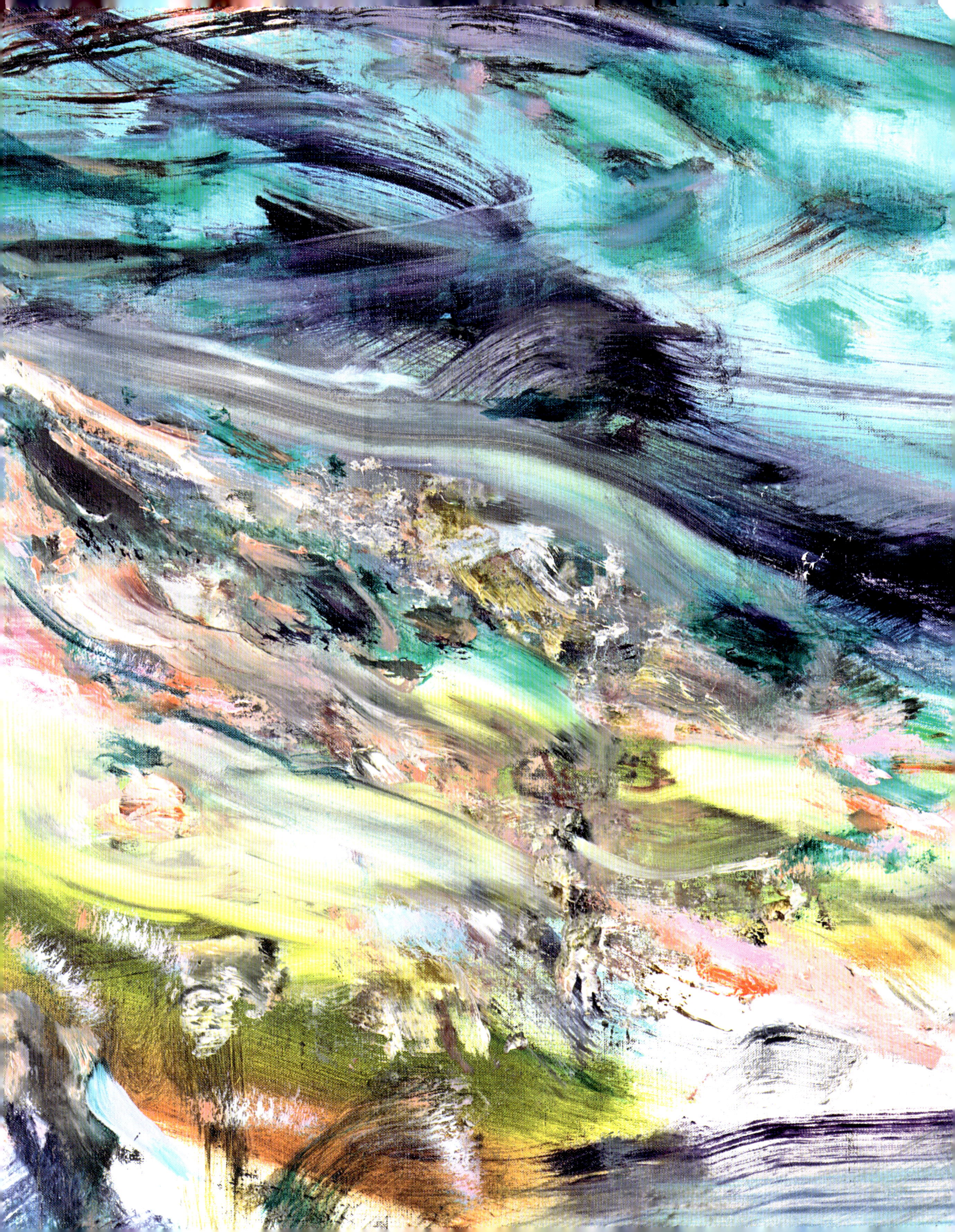

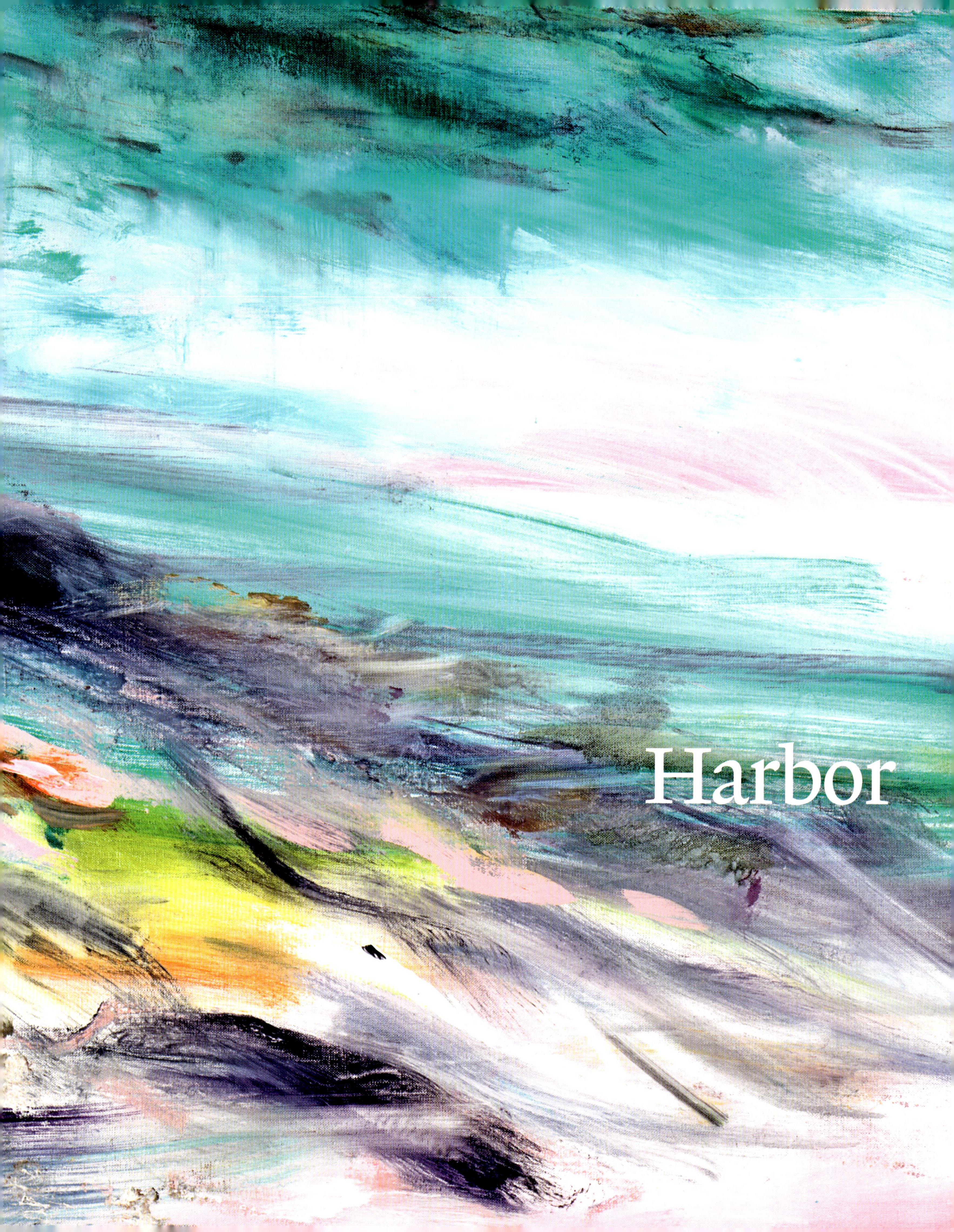
Harbor

Kylie Manning and I met when we were both, it's safe to say, adrift. One afternoon when she joined a group of people I brought to the Metropolitan Museum of Art I heard Manning lucidly explain how Winslow Homer built up paint to, paradoxically, convey depth in *The Gulf Stream* (1899–1906; fig. 1, p. 66). It was revelatory. While writing about Homer in my dissertation, I had read everything there was to read about this painting and had probably spent thousands of hours looking at it, but to have Manning describe his touch with such lucidity changed everything. It wasn't simply the joy of hearing someone who makes art tell me what they know—I now realize Manning was highlighting in Homer what has been one of her abiding concerns as an artist: the oscillation between figure and ground, liquid and solid, land and water, her work and us. Manning establishes these binaries in order to blast them apart.

Ted Barrow

Within weeks of our visit to the Met, Manning invited me to her studio, where she was working on a series of tropical nocturnes that introduced me to her oeuvre. Drawing from her childhood connection to coastal Mexico and using the dynamic lighting of faded family photos of dappled beachfront shacks as her source, these paintings are tenebrist elegies to the strange anxieties and aspirations we hold for the beach (see figs. 2–3, p. 66). In them, palm trees are exotic avatars of longing, simultaneously inscribing legible landscape elements onto otherwise deeply satisfying abstract compositions flecked with dark drama.

We spoke more of Homer and Manning's connection to the coast. The awesome draw of maritime themes has been a lifelong interest for Manning, who worked as a commercial fisherman to pay for school and had a master's maritime captain's license for five-hundred-ton vessels. She grew up chasing swells and fish up and down the coasts of Alaska and Mexico, pitching tents, hiking through mountains, and rambling in a van with her siblings and art teacher parents. Paint's radiant language of coagulating colors and lubricious textures constituted her queer sensory education of the world, a constant binding together of an ever-shifting backdrop of temperate forests and tropical beaches. She went on to study art in New York and then moved to Germany, where she discovered a consonant family of artists. Leipzig, offering generous resources, a collegial spirit, and its legacy of northern romanticism, might have been a great place for a painter of Manning's talents and temperament, but she moved back to New York. It would have been easy to establish a career in Germany, but New York offered her the promise of struggle and the ever-present sublime that few can resist.

Many conversations we had at her studio in front of her landscapes from 2017–18 were about us finding our own place as friends in New York: a place that gains its power as an idea through comparison to everything else around it. Picking back up on that aforementioned push-and-pull of Manning's work, I also add that all of her works, including

66

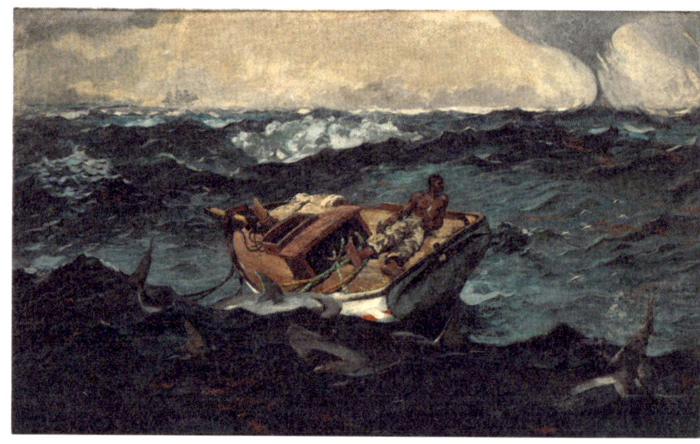

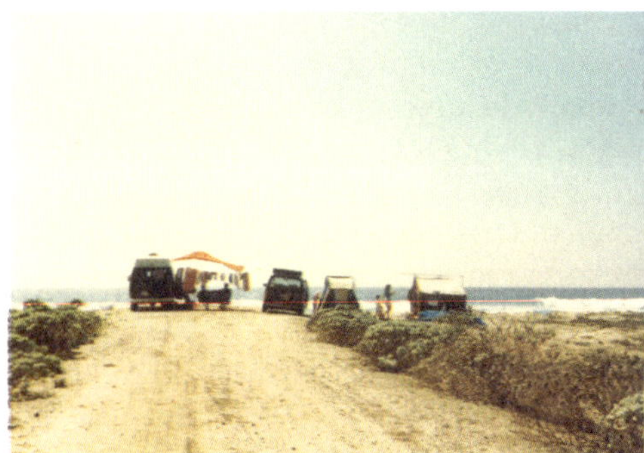

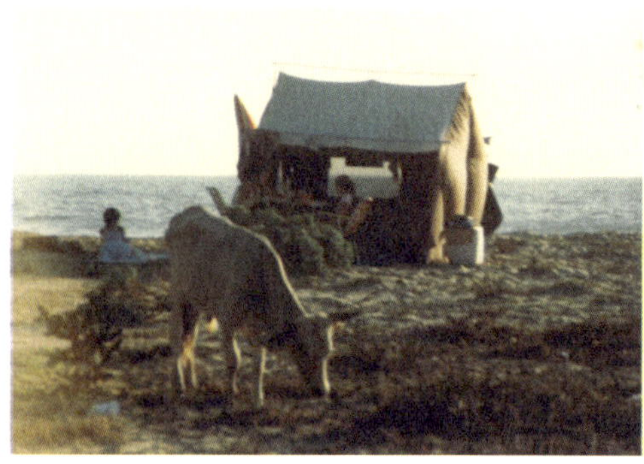

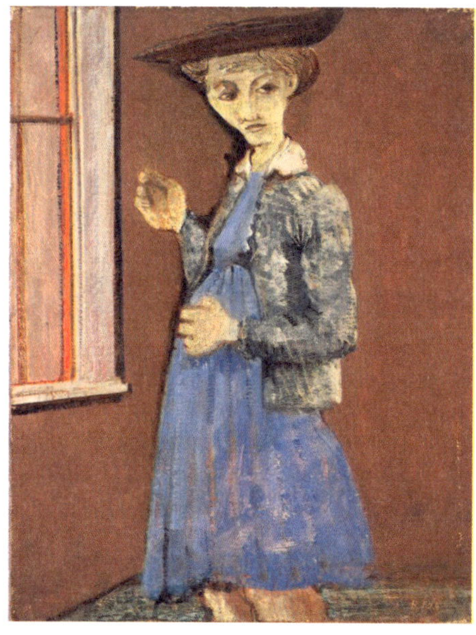

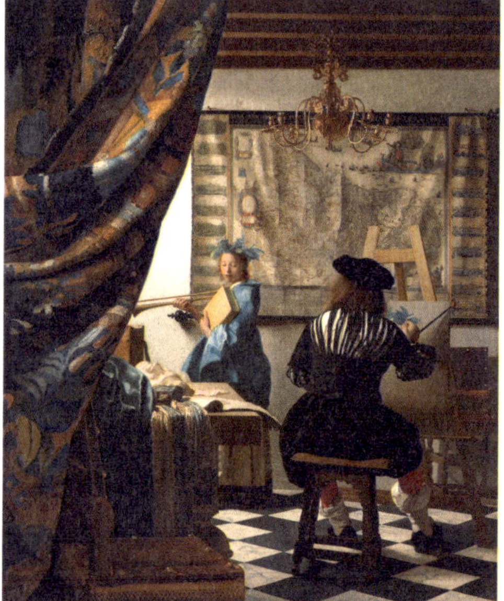

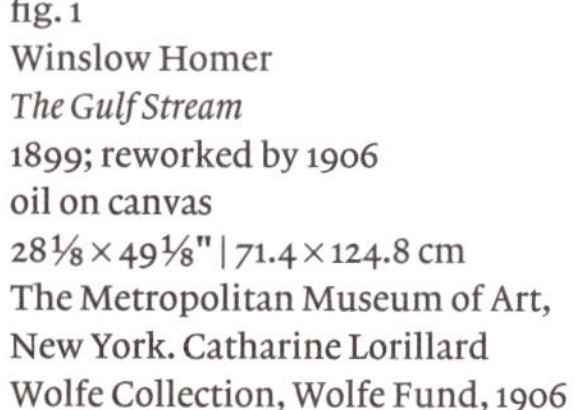

fig. 1
Winslow Homer
The Gulf Stream
1899; reworked by 1906
oil on canvas
28⅛ × 49⅛" | 71.4 × 124.8 cm
The Metropolitan Museum of Art,
New York. Catharine Lorillard
Wolfe Collection, Wolfe Fund, 1906

figs. 2–3
Kylie Manning's family photos
from Baja Sur.

fig. 4
Mark Rothko
Portrait of Mary
1938–39
oil on canvas
36 × 28⅛" | 91.4 x 71.4 cm
©1998 Kate Rothko Prizel and
Christopher Rothko Artist Rights
Society (ARS), New York

fig. 5
Johannes Vermeer
The Art of Painting
c. 1666–68
oil on canvas
47¼ × 39⅜" | 120 × 100 cm
Kunsthistorisches Museum,
Vienna

the ones painted for her 2024 exhibition *Sea Change* at Pace in Hong Kong, draw from elsewhere, like any good experience of the urban. They owe their moments of greatest intensity, foremost their creation in the studio, to the city itself. What I did not know then but appreciate now is that the work that I encountered in her studio at that first meeting came from one of her periods of purge: a palette-cleansing exercise wherein she banishes any bodily presence from her work, setting a thematic stage from which new ideas will spring. Over the next few years, figures reemerged into the foreground, pinning down the energetic brush strokes of their settings like a peg would a billowing tent.

At first glance, Manning's work recalls the scale and style of the most swaggering of Abstract Expressionist paint-slingers and the swashbuckling bravura of Neo-Expressionist figuration. Treating the syncretic pantheon of her influences more as immediate nods to peers than looking over her shoulder to art's historical past, her work might seem inextricable from the pull of New York and the history of its movements. Instead, however, it manages to be about place and still place-less, timely but timeless. David Joselit describes this appeal of the work as "a vertiginous cocktail of futurity in [its] expectation to live on through time, or the evidence of [its] already having done so, while nonetheless proffering an experience of absolute presentness."[1] Drawing on the city's deep currents and traditions, both temporal and topographic, Manning's work is about the assertive intimacy of small groups, yet it is also, like any urban idea, about the yearning for space.

Space is both vast and intimate in Manning's oeuvre. Figures huddle together while gestures bound outward. She works in a controlled frenzy in a studio where the walls are lined with a household of works in progress. The canvases for *Sea Change* face one another, directly or diagonally. A well-aimed, malevolent tennis ball— God forbid   could bounce through her studio, caroming from one painting to another, hitting all five before resting at the end of the room in a pile of thumbed-through monographs.

Think of the paintings in her studio as a feral family, each member with different needs, sharing a different combination of the same genetic makeup, clamoring for attention. "One is the funny one, one is the weird one… but it's important that each painting does not have to show *every* painting's potential… the entire body of work can do that," she says. The paintings are created—"birthed," in her words— together, but they eventually grow apart as a family.

In *Montserrat* (2023; p. 50), a painting raised with this family, described humorously by Manning as the wayward sibling destined to have "gone out into the world into a different kind of place," this push-and-pull between figure and ground becomes palpable. Manning's interrogation of motherhood— her own and, more broadly, how it has been treated in art—manifested through thinking about Mark Rothko at his most figurative, an early work from 1936 titled *Portrait of Mary* (1936; fig. 4) that itself had come out of his riffing on Johannes Vermeer's allegorical *The Art of Painting* (1666–68; fig. 5). What Manning mined from this relay between artists across time was manifold. First, she recognized Rothko's distillation of Vermeer's woman by the window into his own Mary, with all of the vulgate and biblical associations of maternity. Second, working from photographs, she posed with her own baby, Quinn, in an attitude that reverses Vermeer's seated *rückenfigur*, fusing the creation of art and motherhood into one squirrely burst of paint that emanates from the lap of her outlined form. Finally, like the map in the background of Vermeer's *The Art of Painting* or the window that Rothko places beside Mary, the variegated system of interwoven strokes, stains, spatters, and splashes around the figure bespeak a world that is stridently *out*side the studio.

Such references to old masters—Dutch Baroque or New York Modernist—are not the main point, but a matrix through which Manning passed in order to arrive where we meet her, in front of the painting. Just as art can be timeless yet timely, of its time and about time itself, art history also re-animates when deftly referenced. As she told writer Katie White, "Seeing powerful art in New York is the

1
David Joselit, *Art's Properties* (Princeton: Princeton University Press, 2023), xvii.

closest I can get to the experience of being in nature."[2] That lost time and vast space of the wilderness is what she is after in the studio. "It is how my bones are built," she replied recently, when I asked what these art historical references meant to her.

No matter how many calculated decisions (where to make marks, where to rub them out, how to let the blur of erasure on canvas have its own additive presence), and however many thoughts these decisions may spark on the part of the audience, painting might more aptly be another form of dreaming for Manning. She draws from long-buried memories, fragmentary hints of a story otherwise sublimated whose only form is her paintings themselves. However, these lasting impressions also transcend dreams, which may have great depth when we are in them but seldom survive as more than fleeting images and fading feelings when we wake.

Sigmund Freud's theory of condensation applies to the dreamlike nature of Manning's practice, wherein one figure can stand in for more than one possible character in a dream, in a place that is both the city and the woods. Are we ever one gender in our dreams? Are these assignments ever the main point? Manning's rootless images revive notions of home and homesickness that feel like *unheimlich* afterimages. We recognize and locate ourselves in her paintings, the way we feel at home outside our bodies in dreams. Because she learned to paint before she discerned her own gender, this othered self has been an enduring *topos* of Manning's work: bodies that fold into one another, friends as models posing after her own family photos, paintings that recall a dream more felt than seen, fusing many coasts. Manning paints novel pictures that feel familiar.

Indeed, the Prussian blues and browns of *Jetsam* (2023, p. 8) recall John Singer Sargent's ravishing watercolor sketches, like The Worcester Museum's *Bathers* (1917; fig. 6). Comparing each, we see how both artists quickly build bodily forms out of deft strokes precisely placed in eloquent scumbles, how they playfully oscillate between the potential of paint to withhold or reveal. There are parts where we pine for empathy. Hands, legs, faces, and shoulders hook us, while the background dissolves into expressive stains and washes as strokes veer toward an abstract but satisfying formal order. Both artists foreground androgyny, locating their work within a world of queer alterity where identities are as fixed as vapor.

The two artists also share the strategy of allusive art historical references as a ludic game. Painting at the end of the nineteenth century, Sargent mined past art as a potent repository for current motifs. According to Bruce Redford, he posed his sitters in attitudes that made ironic allusions to past portraits, from Van Dyck to Ingres, to evince their awkward contemporaneity.[3] So, too, does Manning. In *Metronome* (2023; p. 32), a rhythmic row of kneeling figures evokes Paul Cézanne's *The Large Bathers* (1900–06; fig. 7), while their bodies have something of the ropy musculature and expressive appendages of Matthias Grünewald. Looking closely, we sense that these kneeling figures are road-weary and graceless in their repose. Knees don't bend; they twist. Distended heels quiver over the ball of a flexed foot. Each calm grouping of huddled figures can simultaneously be read as a buzzing study of a charged tension that is almost electric. Shins and thighs don't so much bend at the knees as zigzag from the hips. The kneeling figure to the right looks toward the audience with an inscrutable gaze. Seen one way, eye contact is an invitation, seen otherwise, a confrontation. Either way, we are granted the space and time to decide how we might relate to these fishy, diffident specters.

Because Manning develops her works in tandem in the studio, each painting plays off another (see fig. 6). Passages of paint and even pigment are threaded through each gesture like strands of DNA. This simply has to do with how they're made: The same color might be read as quiet and cold in one painting and broiling with warmth in another. Individual motifs are built up from their own context in each painting, based on what Manning describes as their "communication." Giving form to binary pairings like "wet/dry," "cold/hot," "dripping/ directing," and "cutting in/backing out," paint that is thinned on the top layer may end up bleeding into

2
Katie White, "Rising-Star Painter Kylie Manning on Her Unlikely New Collaboration with the Ballet Choreographer Christopher Wheeldon," *Artnet News*, May 12, 2023, https://news.artnet. com/art-world/ kylie-manning-nyc- ballet-pace-geneva- 2299497.

3
Bruce Redford, *John Singer Sargent and the Art of Allusion* (New Haven: Yale University Press, 2016).

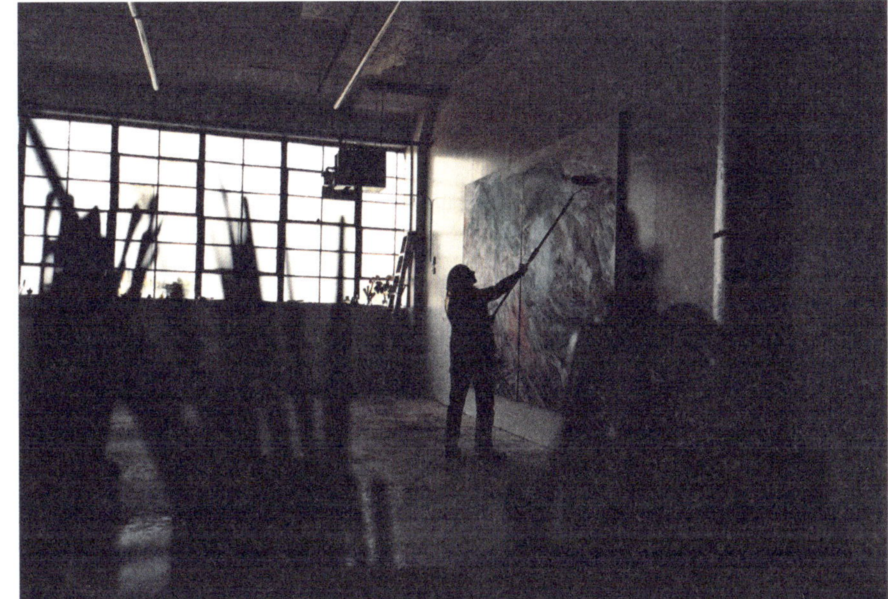

6

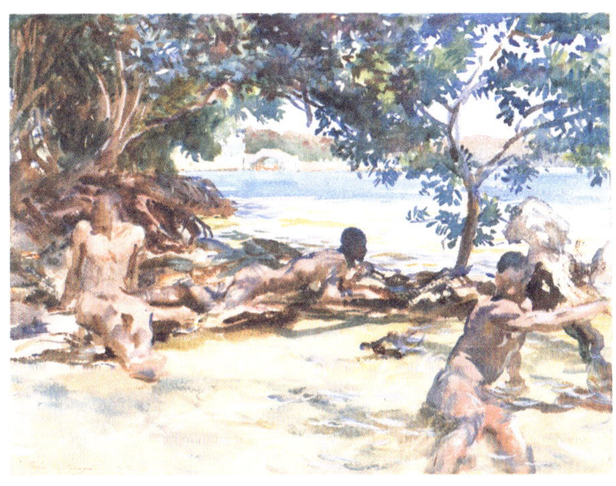

7

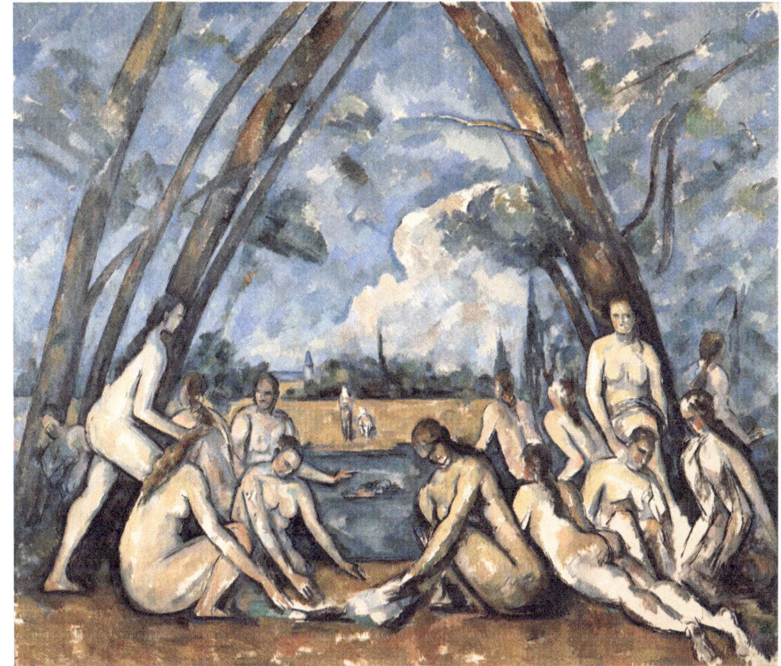

8

fig. 6
Manning in her studio, Queens,
New York.

fig. 7
John Singer Sargent
Bathers
1917
oil on canvas
15¾ × 20¾" | 40 × 53 cm
Worcester Art Museum, Massachusetts.
Sustaining Membership Fund

fig. 8
Paul Cézanne
The Large Bathers
1900–06
oil on canvas
6'10⅞ × 8'2¾" | 210.5 × 250.8 cm
Philadelphia Museum of Art. Purchased
with the W. P. Wilstach Fund, 1937

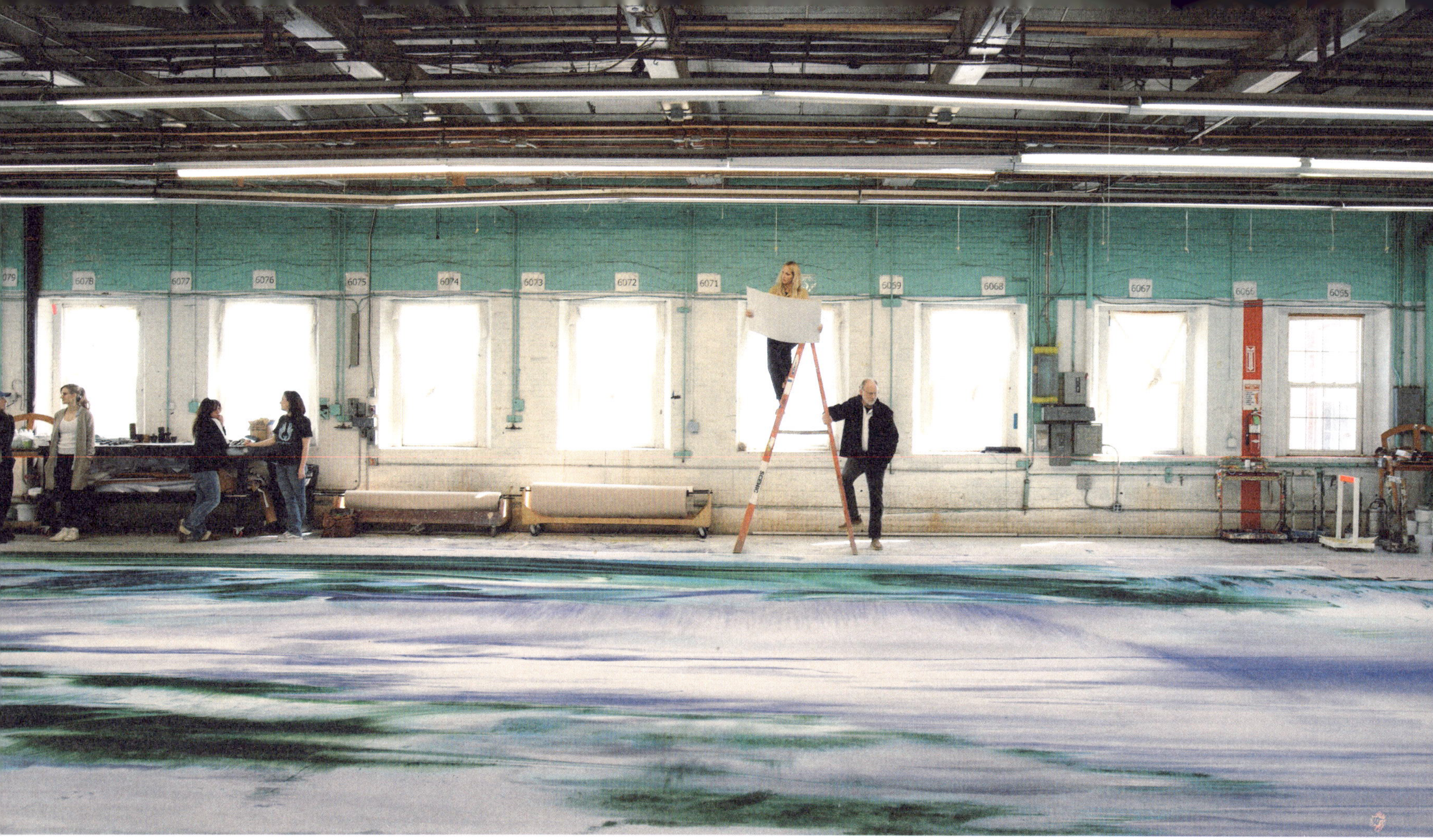

fig. 9
Manning supervising backdrop
creation for Christopher Wheeldon's
From You Within Me.

figs. 10–11
(pp. 72–73, 76–77)
Installation views, *Both Sides Now*,
Pace Gallery, Los Angeles, 2022.

fig. 12 (p. 74)
Kylie Manning
King Tide (detail)
2023
oil on linen
60 × 84" | 152.4 × 213.4 cm

fig. 13 (p. 75)
Kylie Manning
Moonglow (detail)
2022
oil on linen
74⅛ × 96⅛" | 188.3 × 244.2 cm

the layer below. It is never one thing, but is everything, everywhere, at all times. The process of painting is both alchemical and an act of choreography.

Both Sides Now, Manning's September 2022 debut exhibition with Pace in Los Angeles, grouped her works in a sequence of atmospheric experiences that might be tied to the seasons but also, just as plausibly, might consider our place in the world with an eco-critical probe (see figs. 10–11). The art historian in me wanted to connect her work from 2022 to Alexandre Evariste Fragonard's late, great *Progress of Love* (1771–73) sequence at The Frick Collection, as well as Thomas Cole's *Course of Empire* (1833–36) across Central Park at the New York Historical Society. But Manning's work is far too slippery and complex to be pinned down to the over-determined plots of these eighteenth- and nineteenth-century forebearers.

Few painters today would confidently fuse together the hot pinks and emerald greens that she does, masterfully combining the newest, radioactive-looking pigments with the most traditional and organic. These Neo-Rococo passages of her work harken back to Fragonard, who summoned the changes of seasons as natural allegories for the stages of a lifelong love: early spring for *The Meeting* at the beginning, winter for *Love Letters* at the end. Paintings like *Sapling* (2022)*, King Tide* (2023; see fig. 12), *Now and Then* (2022), and *Moonglow* (2022; see fig. 13), each with its own temperature and level of address to the audience, connect to a cycle of earthly time, if not simply seasonal passages. As the first in-person opening I had attended since 2019, and with the cumbersome nightmare of the previous year and a half still looming in Los Angeles, *Both Sides Now* recalled Cole's rumination on the end of times, not the beginning. It's not just the landscape format in which Manning's work is staged, but more that her paintings seem to fuse Cole's first "Savage" state of humanity within the landscape of "Desolation" in the last.

Seeing how her work had distilled and re-framed the themes of collective solitude in our current desolate empire underscored for me how we survive through the disconnected intimacy of family and friends, teetering on the edge of a proverbial cliff. Each painting in *Both Sides Now* is a resilient love letter to the tattered communities that are forged through their alterity, an amalgam of Fragonard's palette and Cole's landscapes populated by Manning's emphatic huddles, with the rejected finding comfort in the jetsam.

In the spring of 2023, while pregnant, Manning worked with the choreographer Christopher Wheeldon to stage a ballet at Lincoln Center set to Arnold Schoenberg's *Verklärte Nacht*. Manning designed the costumes and conceived of her paintings as monumental backdrops for the dancers (see fig. 9). This brings to mind early twentieth-century collaborations between Henri Matisse, Pablo Picasso, and Sonia Delaunay with Sergei Diaghilev's Ballets Russes, but we might as well go further back to the tradition of *tableaux vivants* and phantasmagoric productions of the nineteenth century. Conceiving her compositions on a sixty-foot scale, Manning once again purged the figure from her work, as the bodily presence would be mobilized by the ballet dancers themselves. The first painting, *Pareidola* (2023; p. 56), on a sheer, shark-tooth scrim, used transparent areas lit from both behind and in front to recreate what many layers of oil on titanium ground can convey. The first series of choreography was completed with the dancers emerging behind the veil, inside the landscape. The second backdrop, *You into me, me into you* (2023; p. 60), seared through as the first veil lifted, bringing an atmospheric sense of dawn and deep perspective to an otherwise heavy and long night. Seeing Wheeldon's dancers move in front of her backdrops that, for once, made literal the scale to which her paintings usually only allude precipitated a profound shift in her practice.

In *Sea Change* (2023; p. 42), the first time that Manning has used a diptych composition in her work, a torrential landscape writhes between the figures. The diagonal cascade running from the upper left to the lower right isolates one larger bundle of figures from the others on its pendant. Using

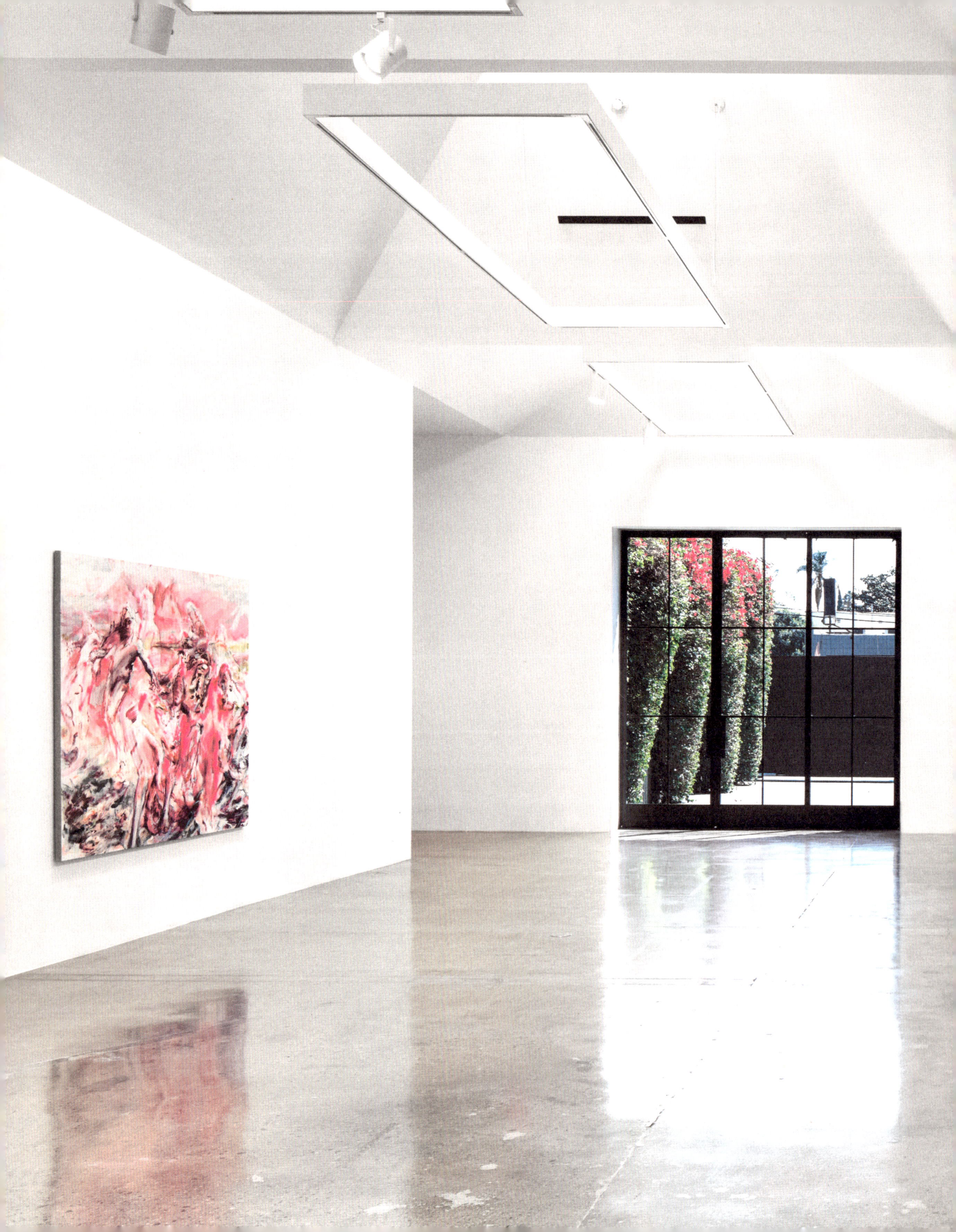

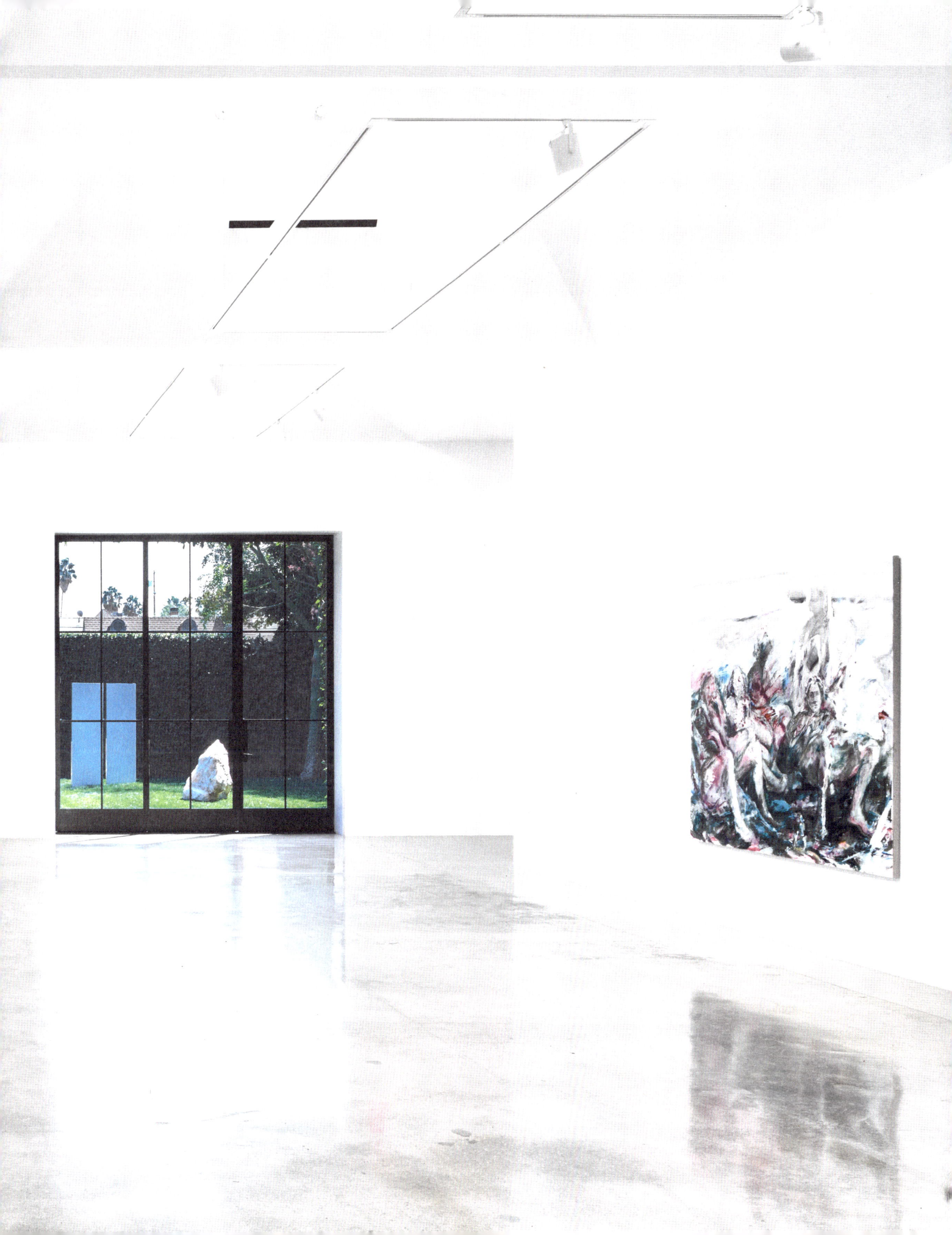

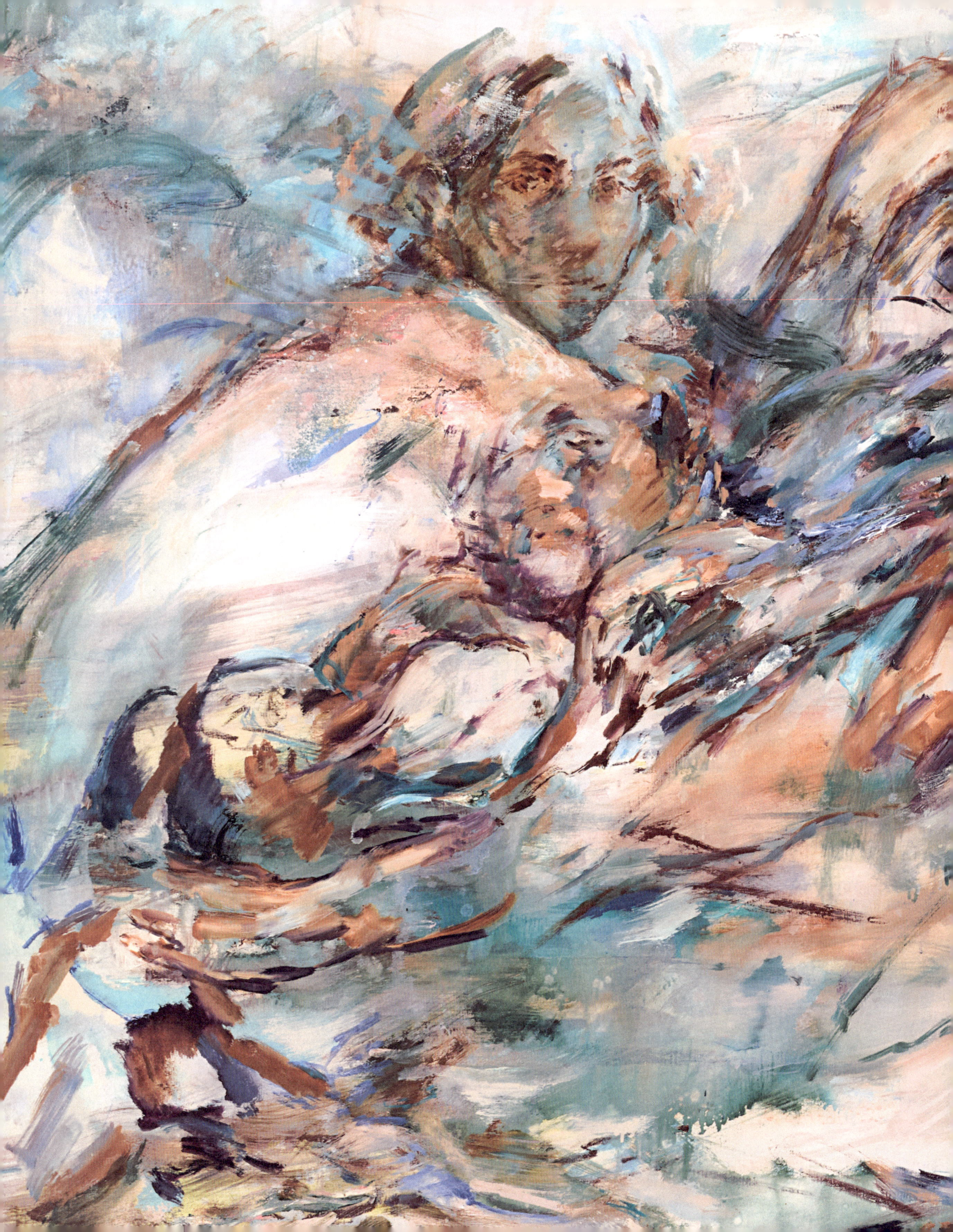

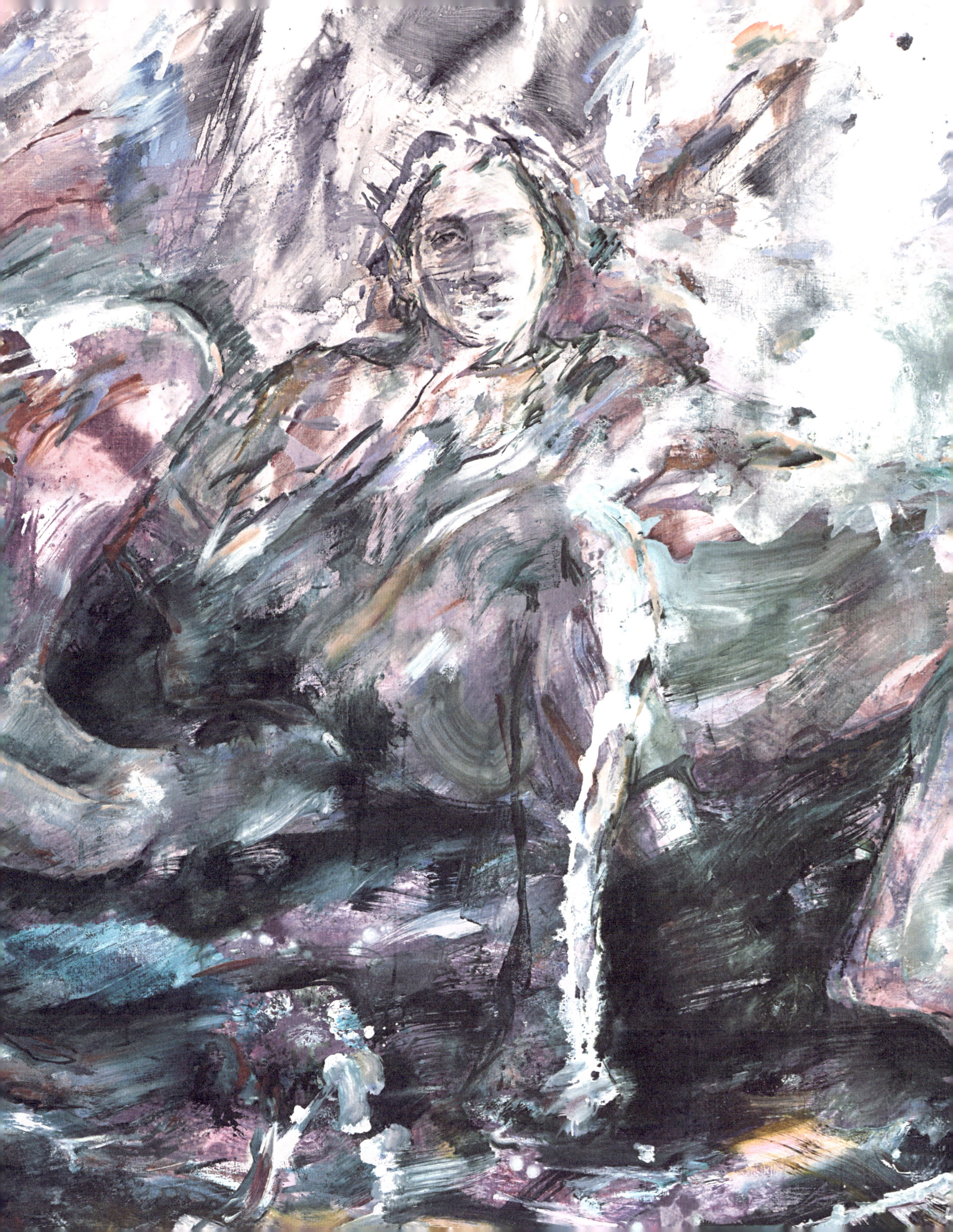

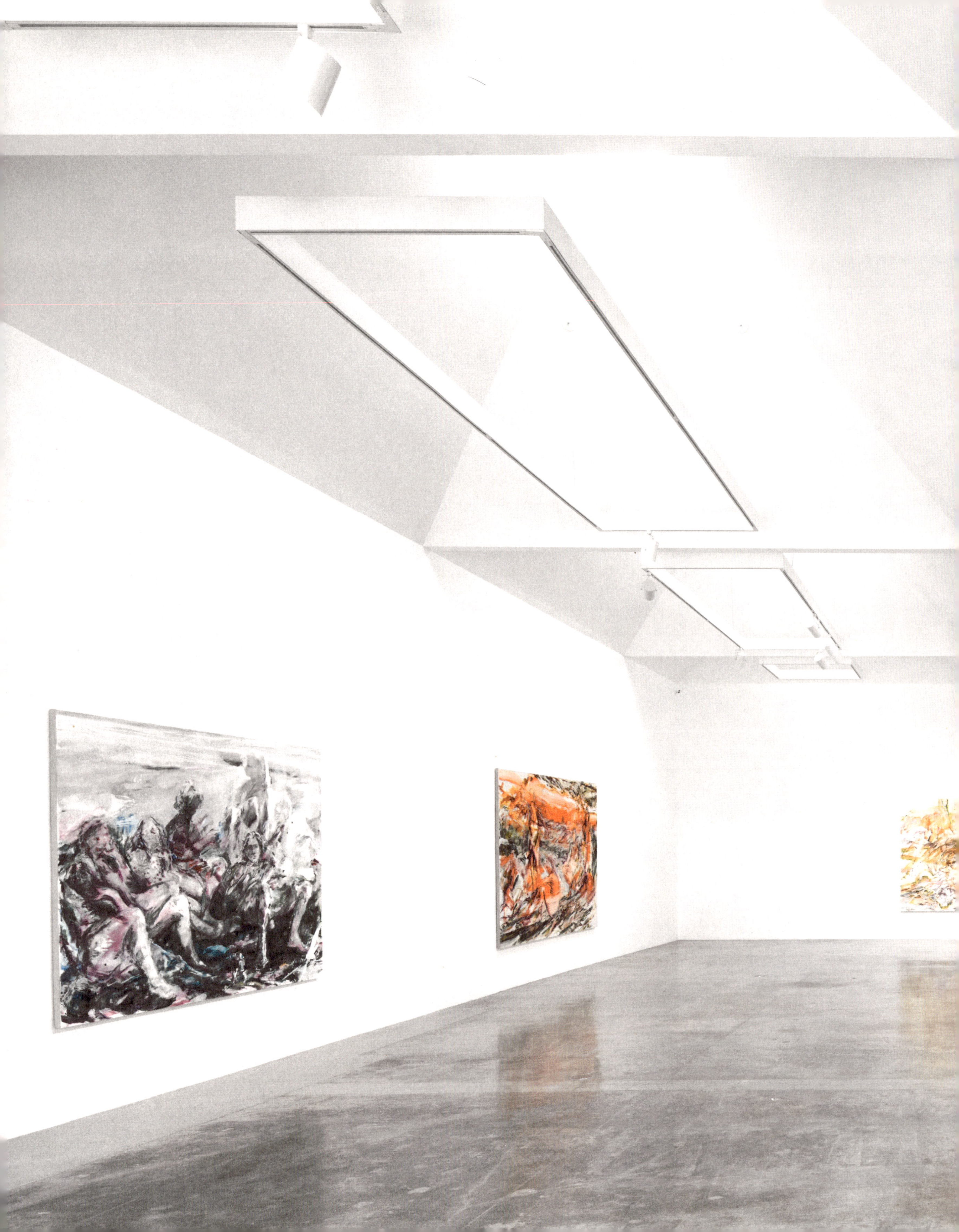

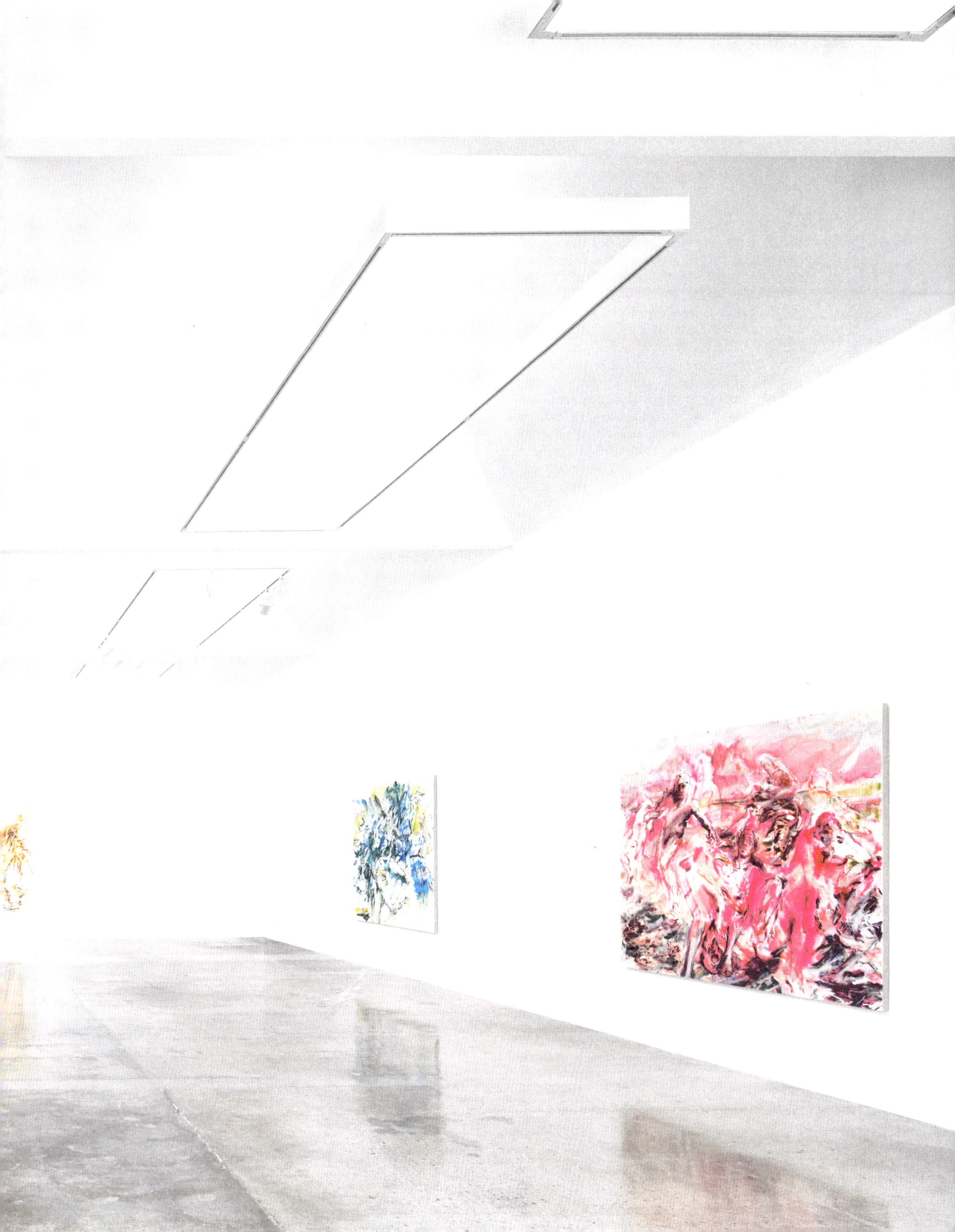

the same diffused, cool blues and ruddy pinks seen in the performance, Manning nonetheless keys up the drama in her figures' contorted and disquieted poses. Though recumbent, they are charged with a foreboding tension, as if the radiant force that pours from top to bottom, though natural, spells dissolution.

On the night of the final performance of *From You Within Me*, Manning's water broke. She was rushed to the hospital and endured, in her words, a "gnarly and harsh birth." Both her own life and her baby's were threatened. She labored for twenty-four hours. Had things gone a different way, her life story may have ended with the ballet's final performance on May 16, 2023. A week later, the family left the hospital; they slowly recovered, got to know one another, and, as soon as she could, Manning returned to the studio, emboldened. One might expect anyone, after such a precipitous rise over the past eighteen months, a ballet, a birth, and a near-death experience, to return tentatively, cautiously recommencing a now anemic version of their past work. But for Manning the exact opposite is true: Just as she has drawn energy from the strain of the city and its unique challenges, she has rebounded into a more powerful and assured practice, galvanized by dramatic upheaval. *Sea Change* doubles the dimensions of her normal work and—dare I say it?—packs twice the punch.

Little Wild Bouquet (2023; p. 20) takes its title from the last lines of Leonard Cohen's 1992 song "Democracy":

> *I'm sentimental, if you know what I mean*
> *I love the country but I can't stand the scene*
> *And I'm neither left or right*
> *I'm just staying home tonight*
> *Getting lost in that hopeless little screen*
> *But I'm stubborn as those garbage bags*
> *That time cannot decay*
> *I'm junk but I'm still holding up this little*
> *wild bouquet*

As we risk losing hope in our countless little screens, the notion of loving the country but being unable to stand the scene continues to feel sharply salient. Now more than ever, we need to engage with art, that stubborn little garbage bag "that time cannot decay," to help us find meaning. Cohen's sentiment stands as a paean to the continual relevance of art outside of the junk of historical time. Great paintings are like that: They rebound from the time and place experienced outside the studio without being tied to a date, pledging promises of futurity. Awash in florid purples and browns, at least three bodies, posed similarly, echo one another across the canvas in a Muybridgean sequence. A rhythm of opaque white splashes and stains skip from a halo-like loop above the head. They expand into a series of broken chevrons that dance to the right. These splashes are risky: They could ruin the whole thing but don't. Instead, they accent the taut graphic figuration below them in a manner that I can't help but think was informed by Manning's expanded experience of her work through multiple layers of scrim and dance in Wheeldon's ballet.

Lurid and warm, Manning's new work is layered with bold strokes and imbued with a deeper sense of life's high stakes and the primacy of art-making. It is not an escape from reality but an immersive celebration of it. Each emphatic bundle of brush strokes and stains, each figure group, each painting alone and in a suite, developed first in her studio, encountered later in the space of a gallery, and then surviving as memory, is this: a wild bouquet of the redemptive pull of color on canvas and all that pushes us back toward it.

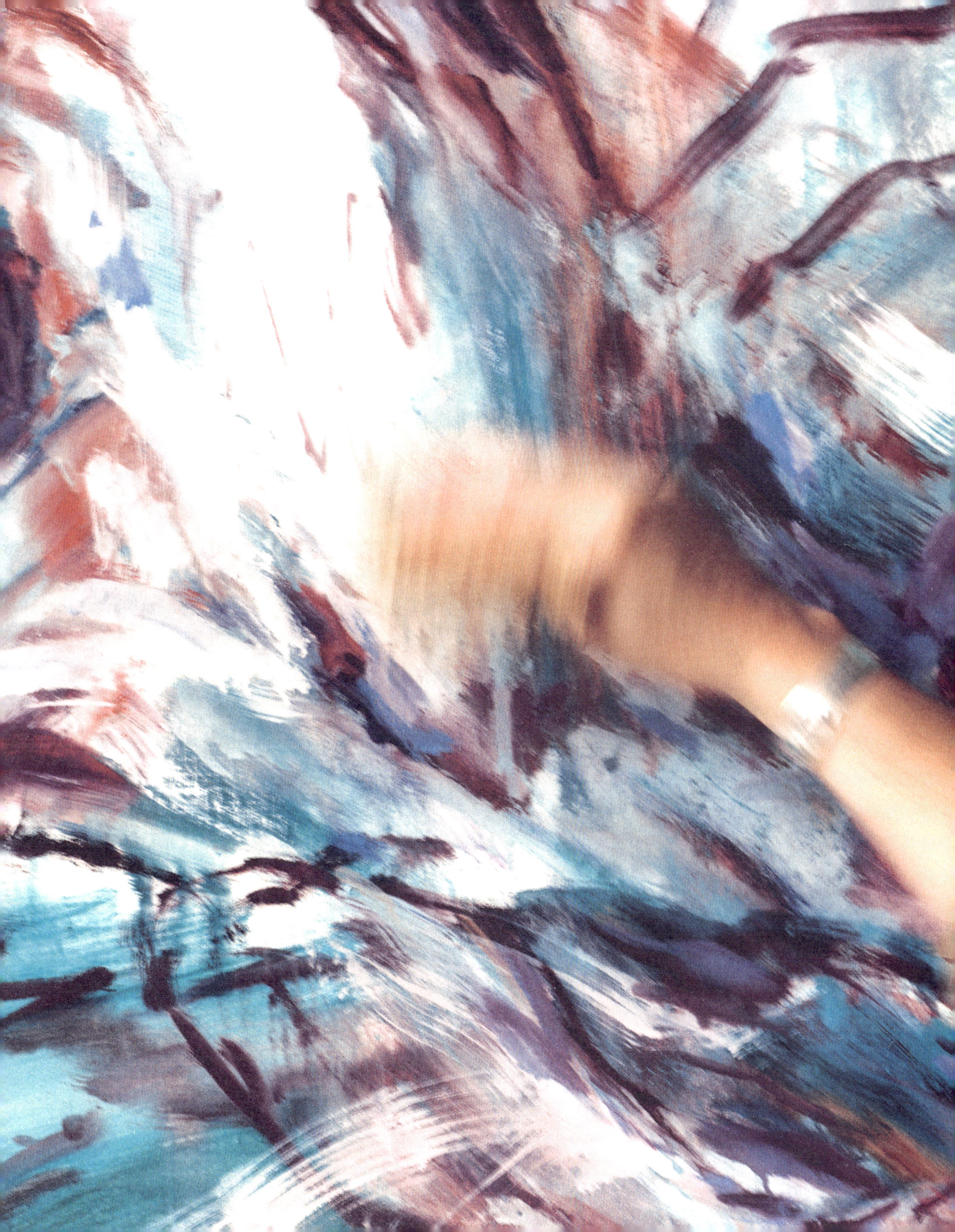

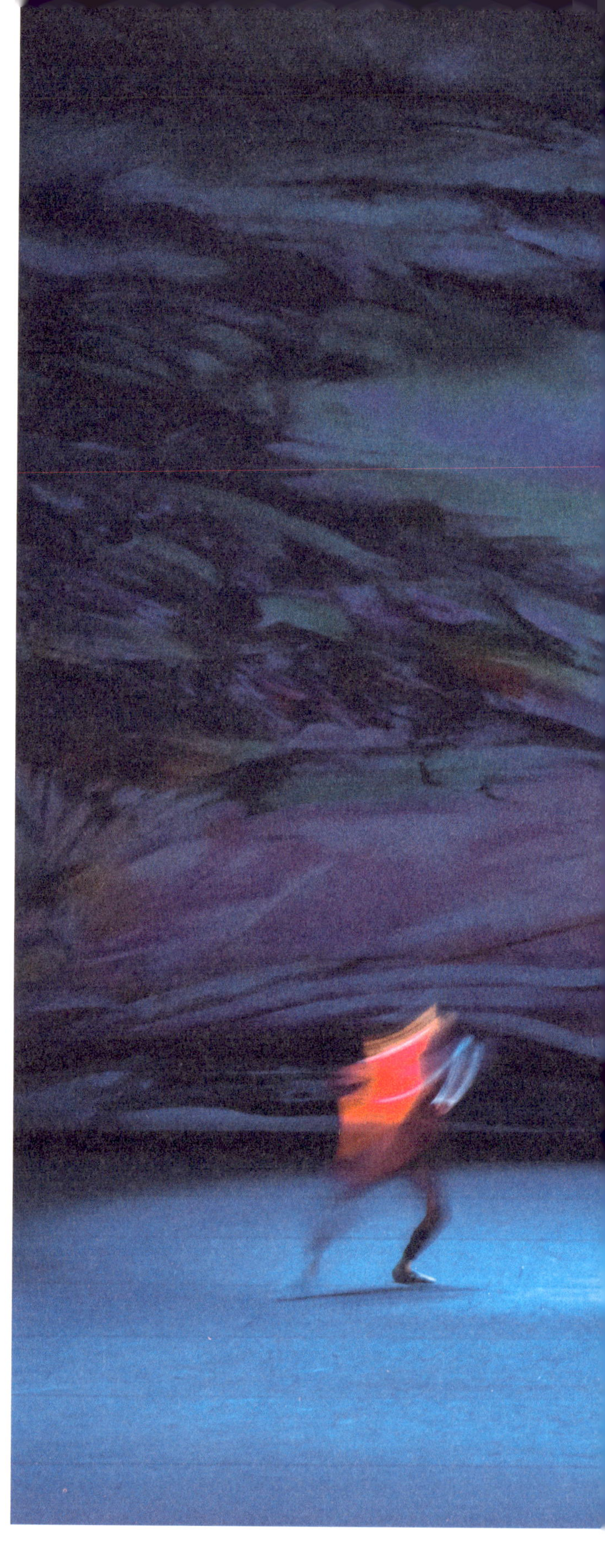

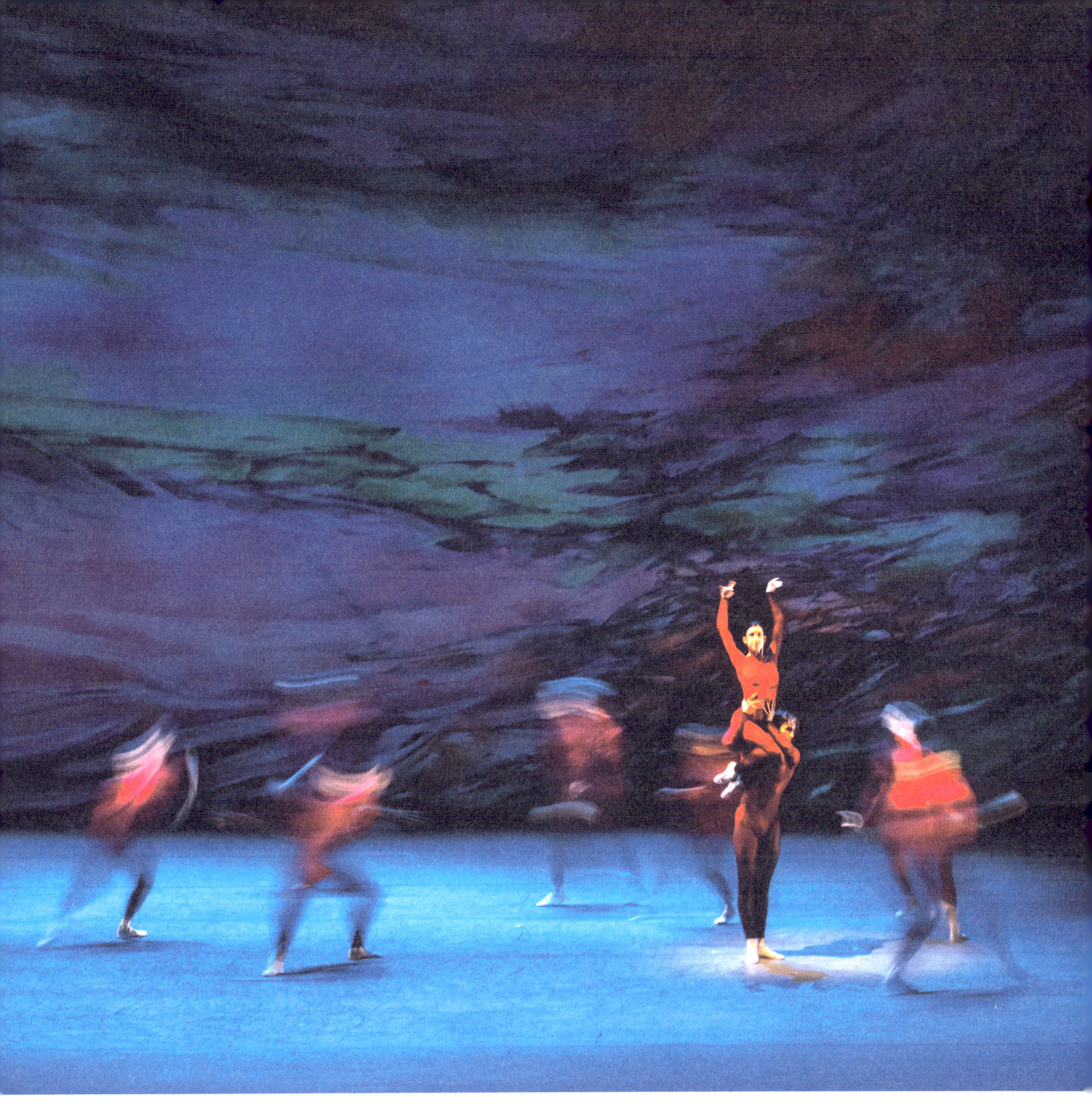

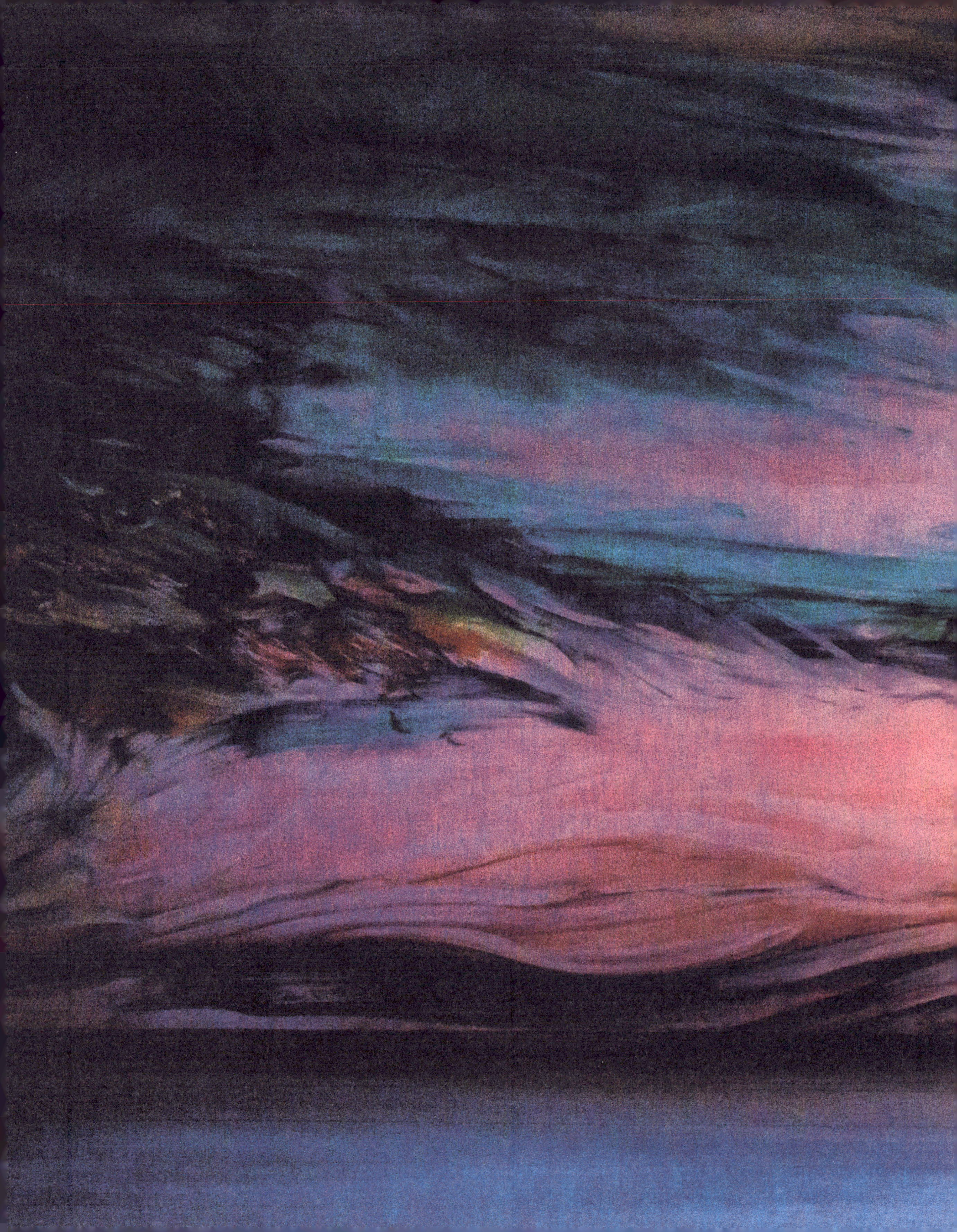

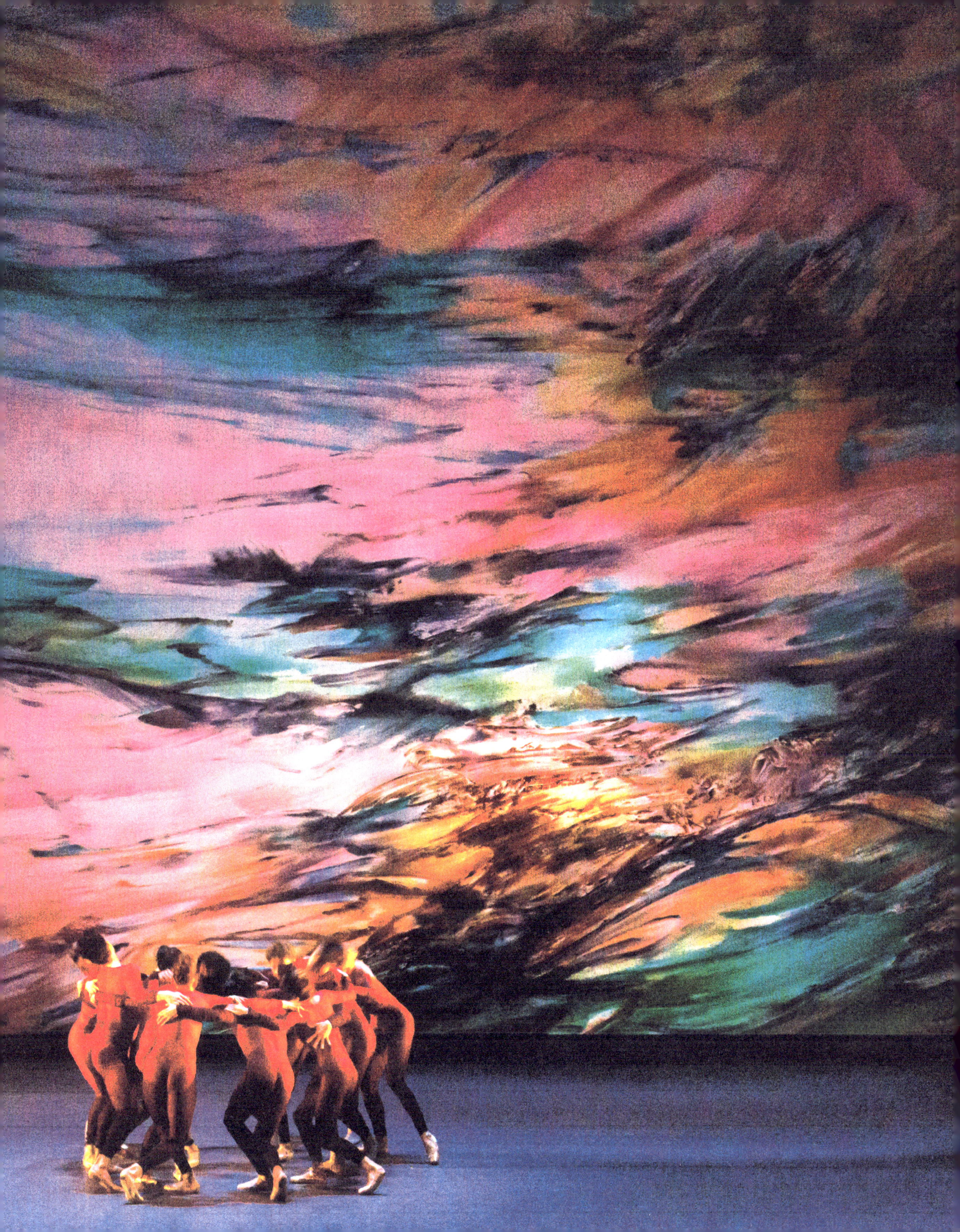

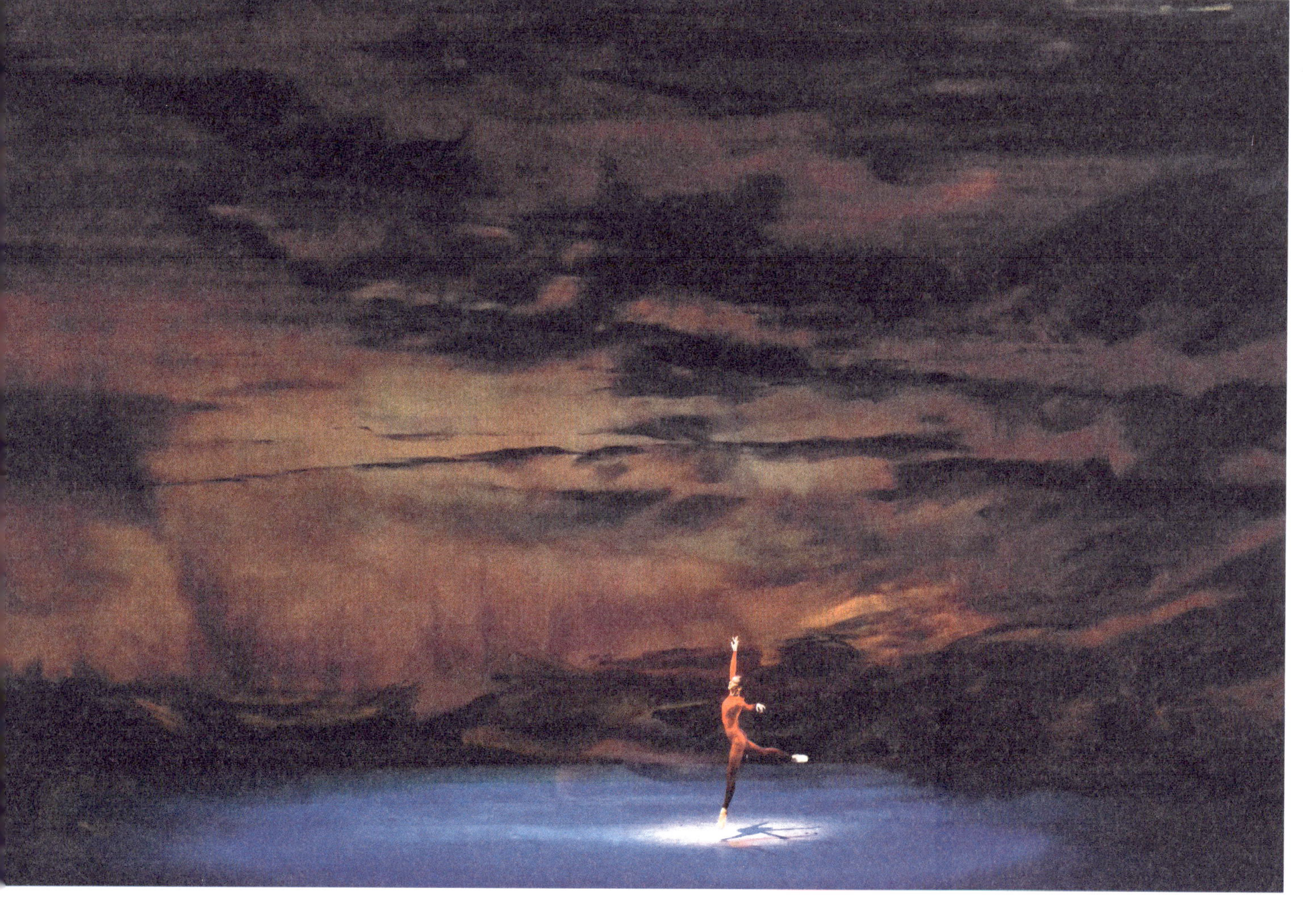

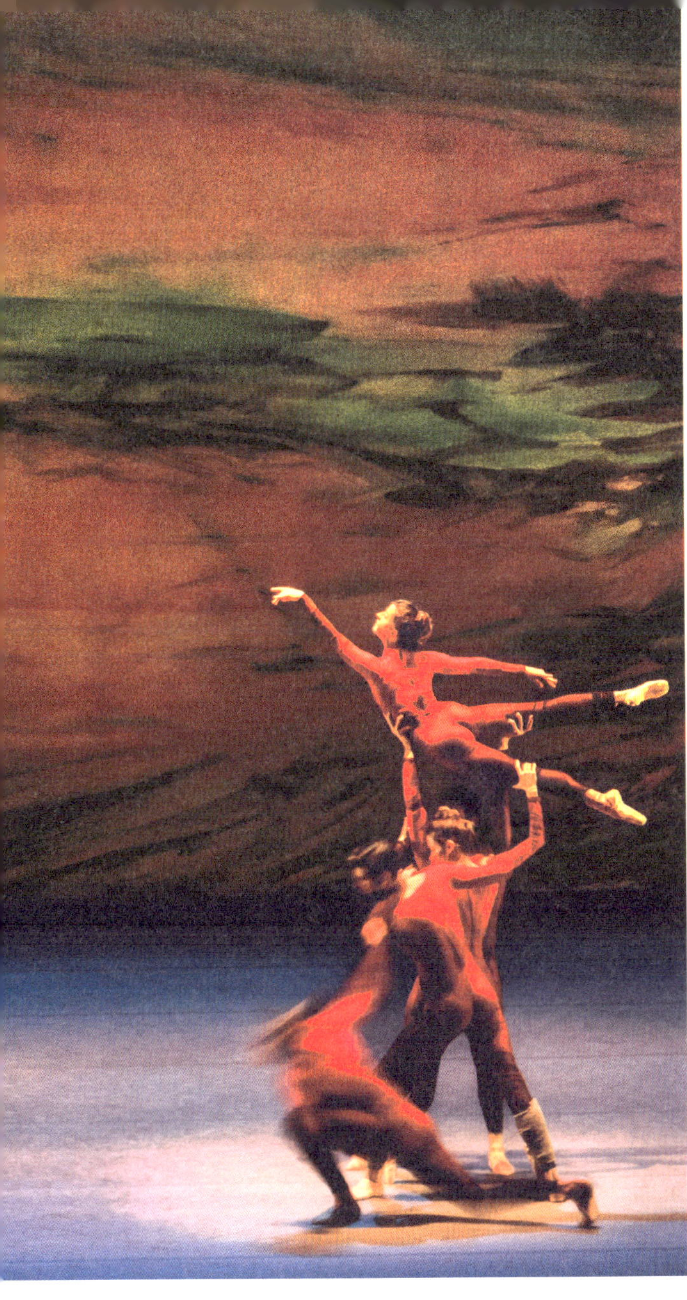

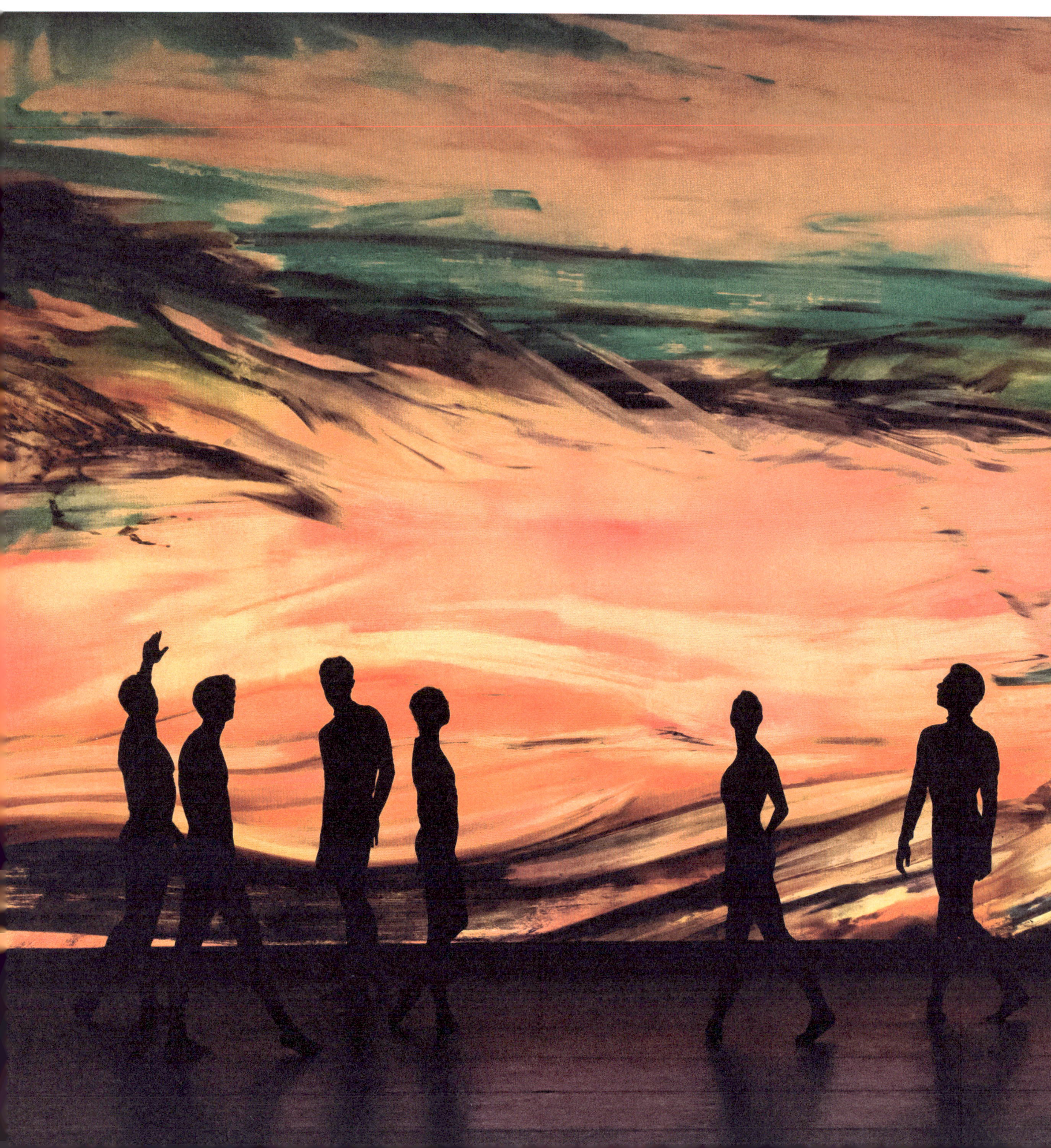

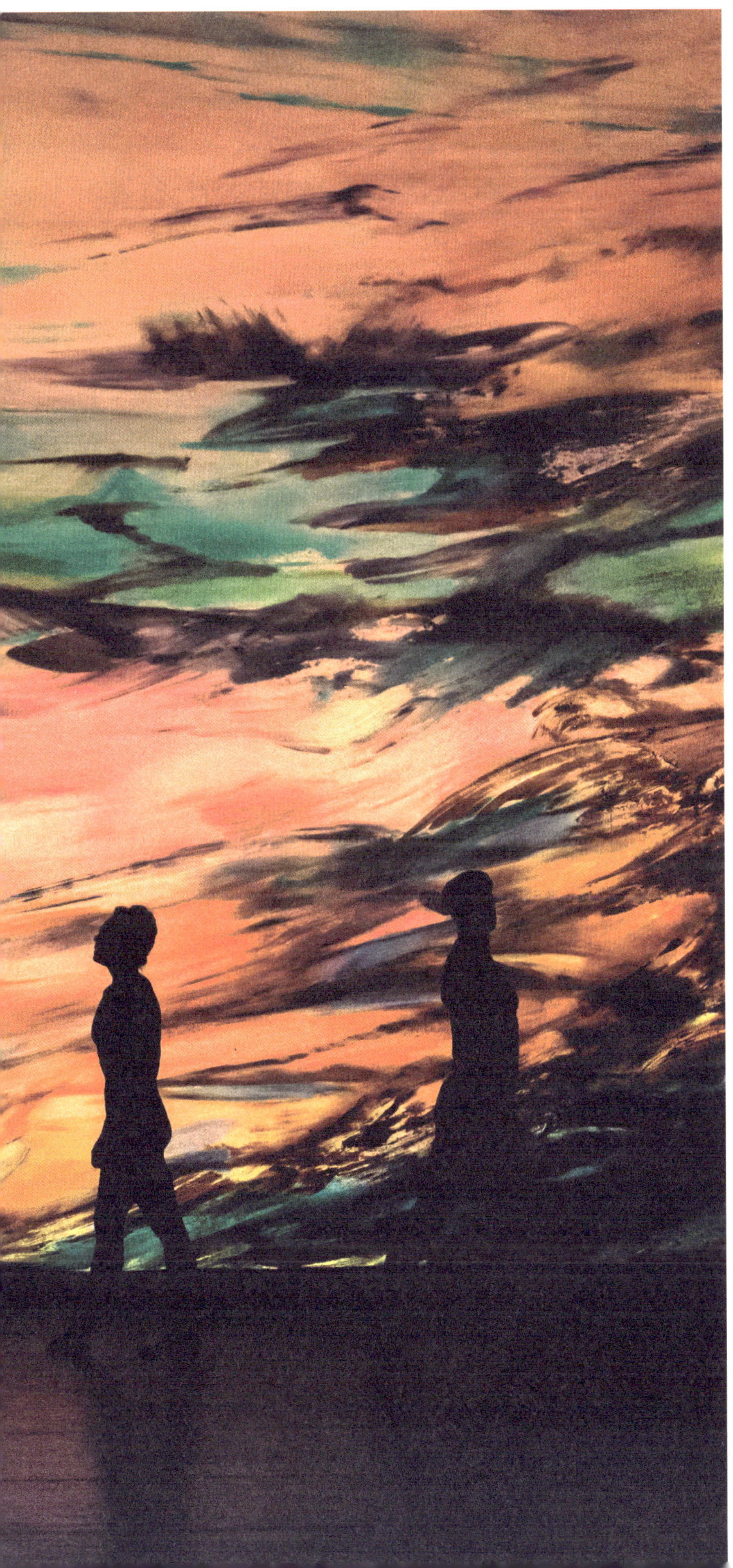

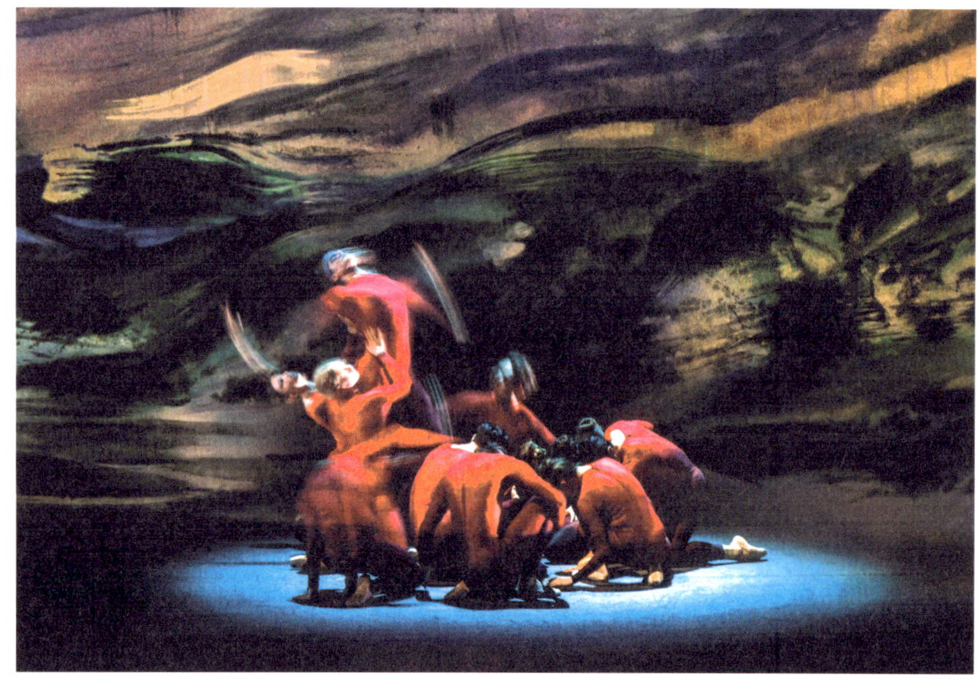

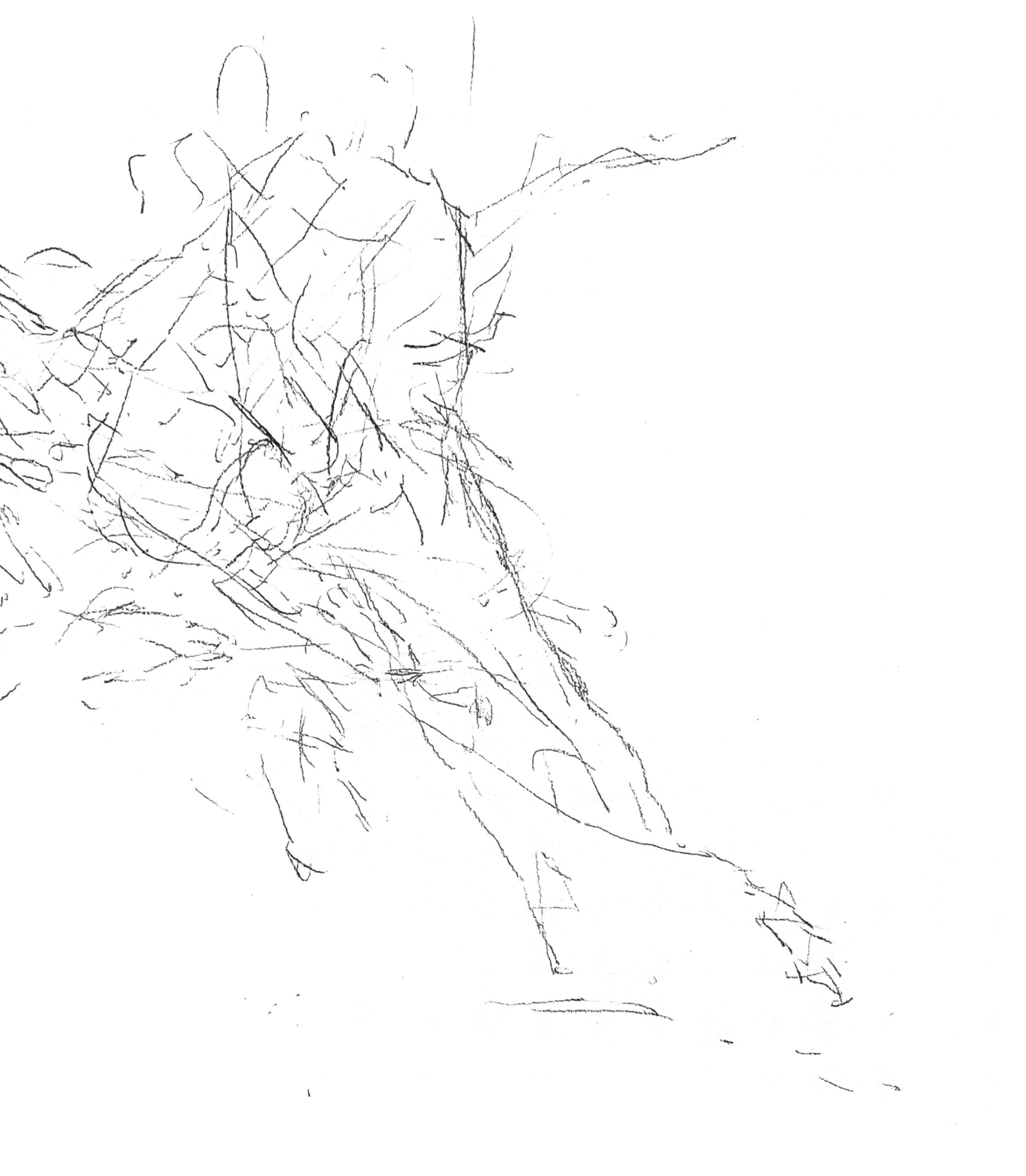

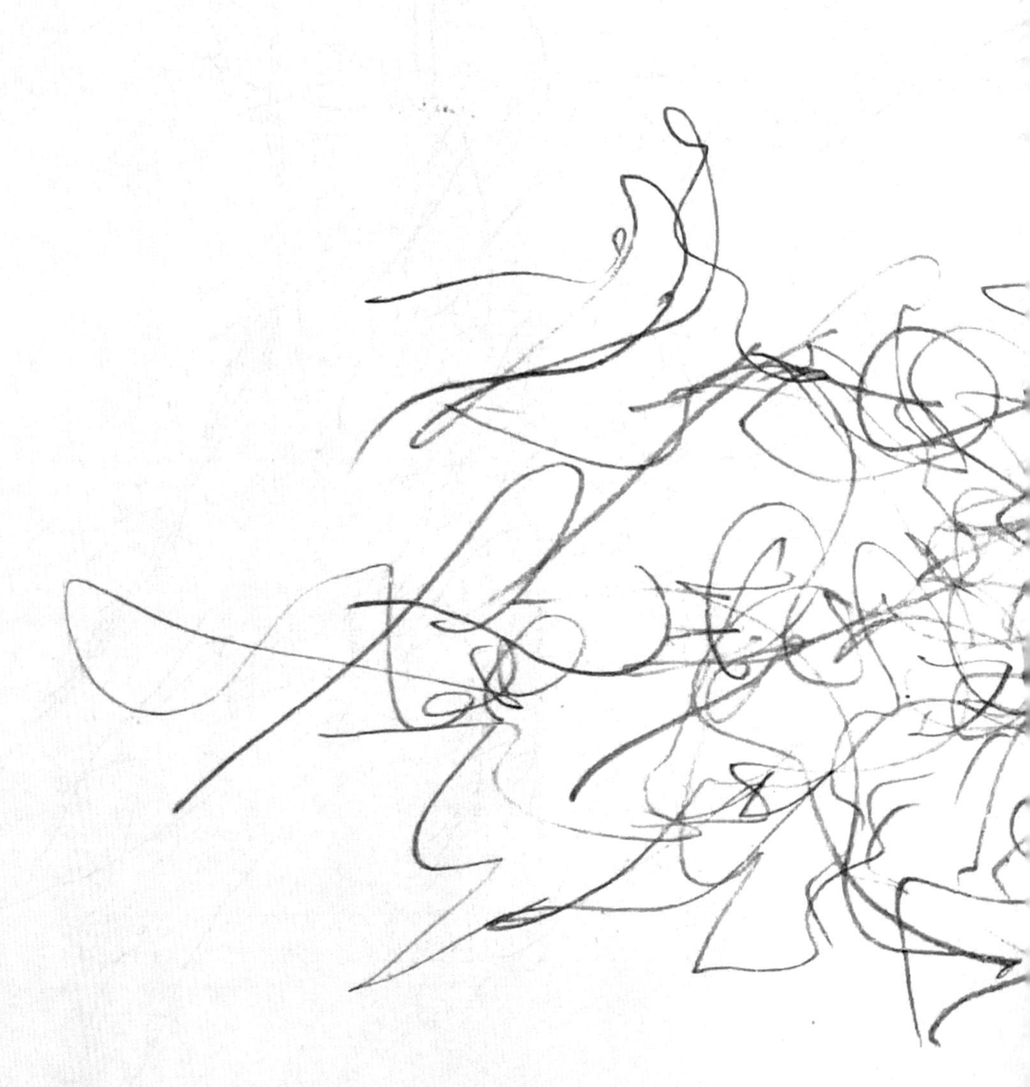

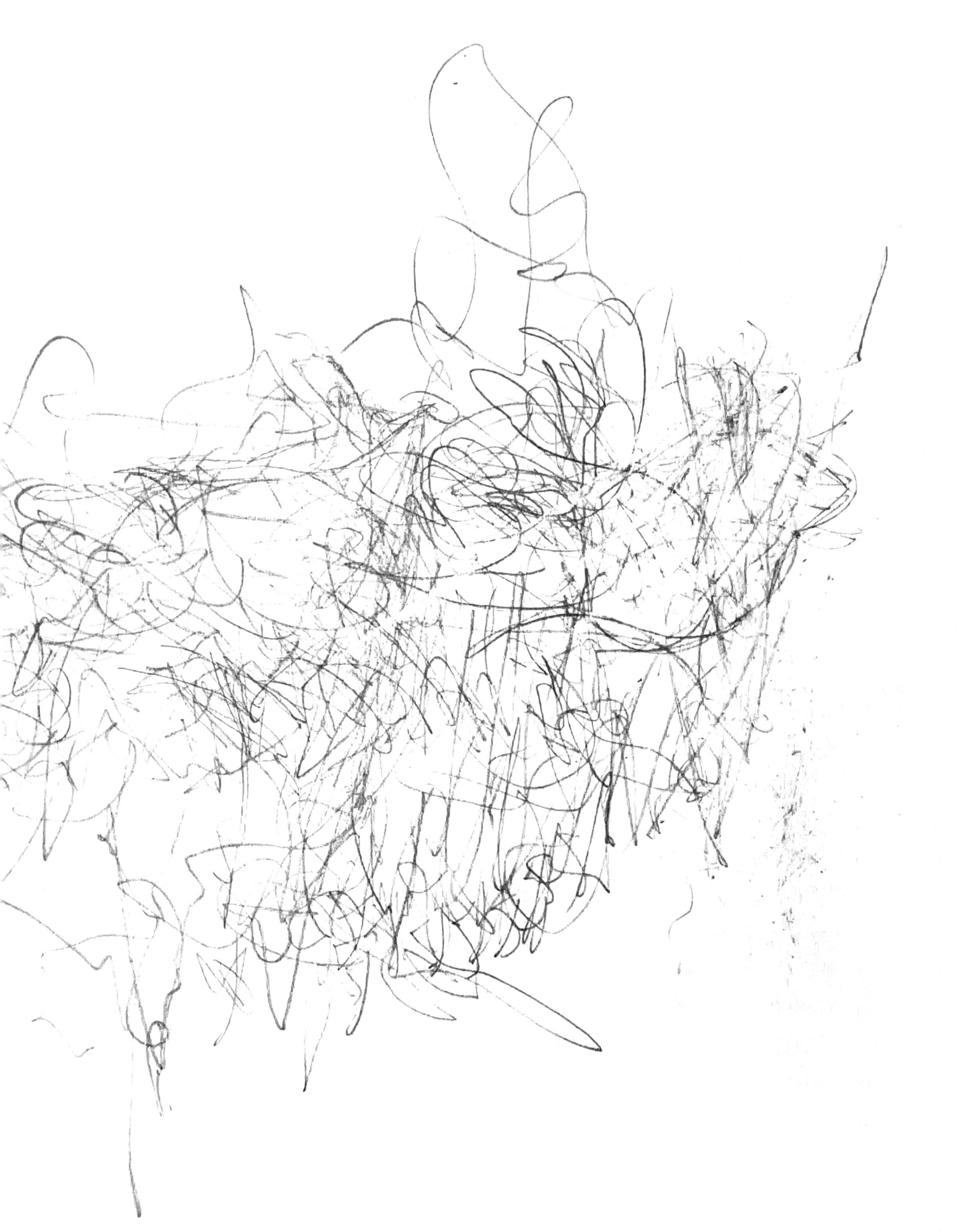

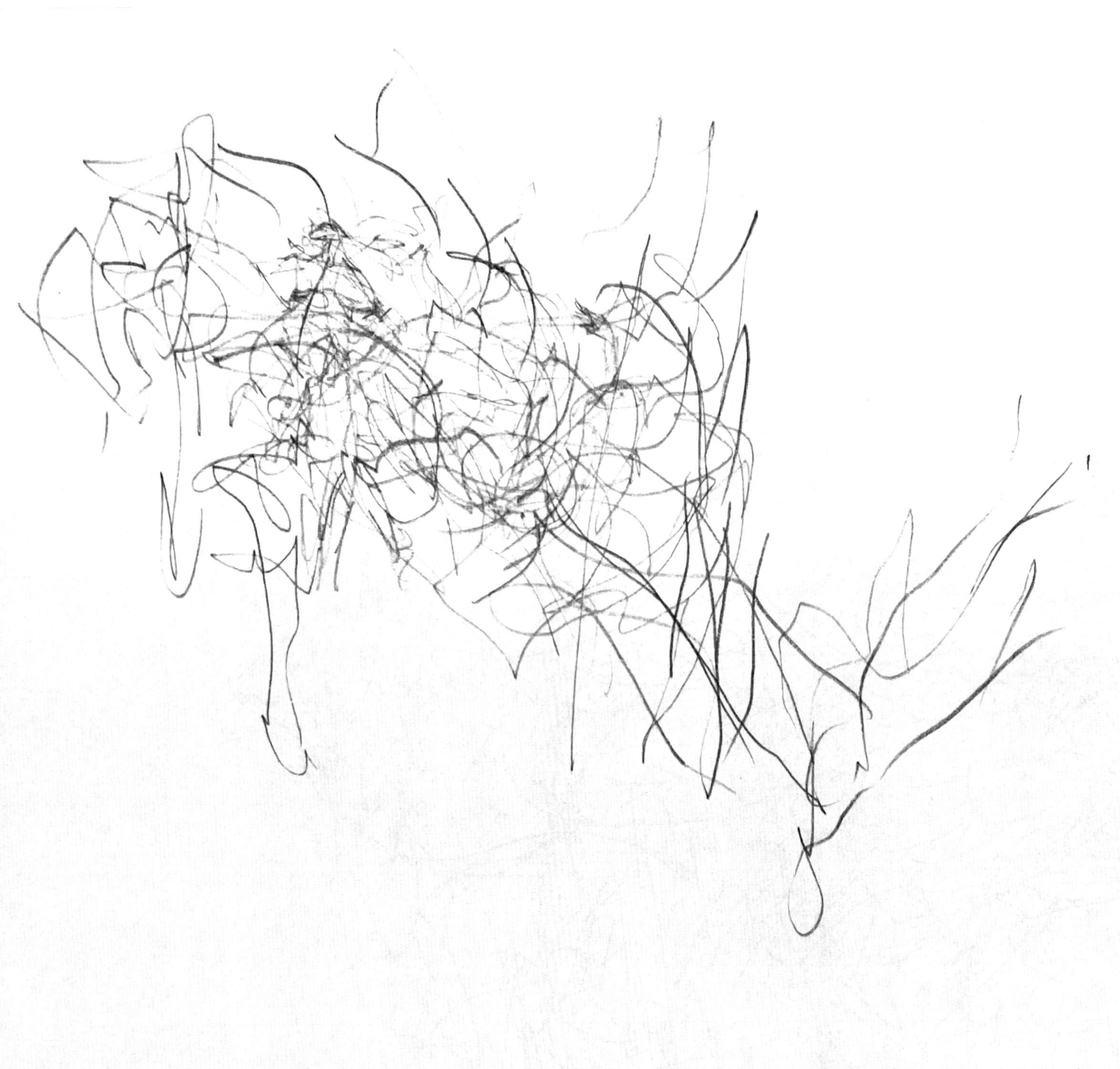

A special thank you to my folks and siblings, for always helping me to see clearly, and to my husband and daughter, who are behind the light and love in every mark. Christiana, the extraordinary publications team, and the entire Pace family, you advocate for artists in such a genuine way, and it means the world to me. Ted, speaking with you about art is one of my greatest joys in my life; your insight is breathtaking. Erin, Joe, and Alex, looking back at these memories through your extraordinary lenses is a great gift. Tristan and Chris, your creative talent and kindness has ruined me for future collaborations. Jing, the sensitivity of your eye is unparalleled; every image is better for it. And finally, Michael, you have brought heart and thoughtfulness to every inch of every page. Thank you.
—Kylie Manning

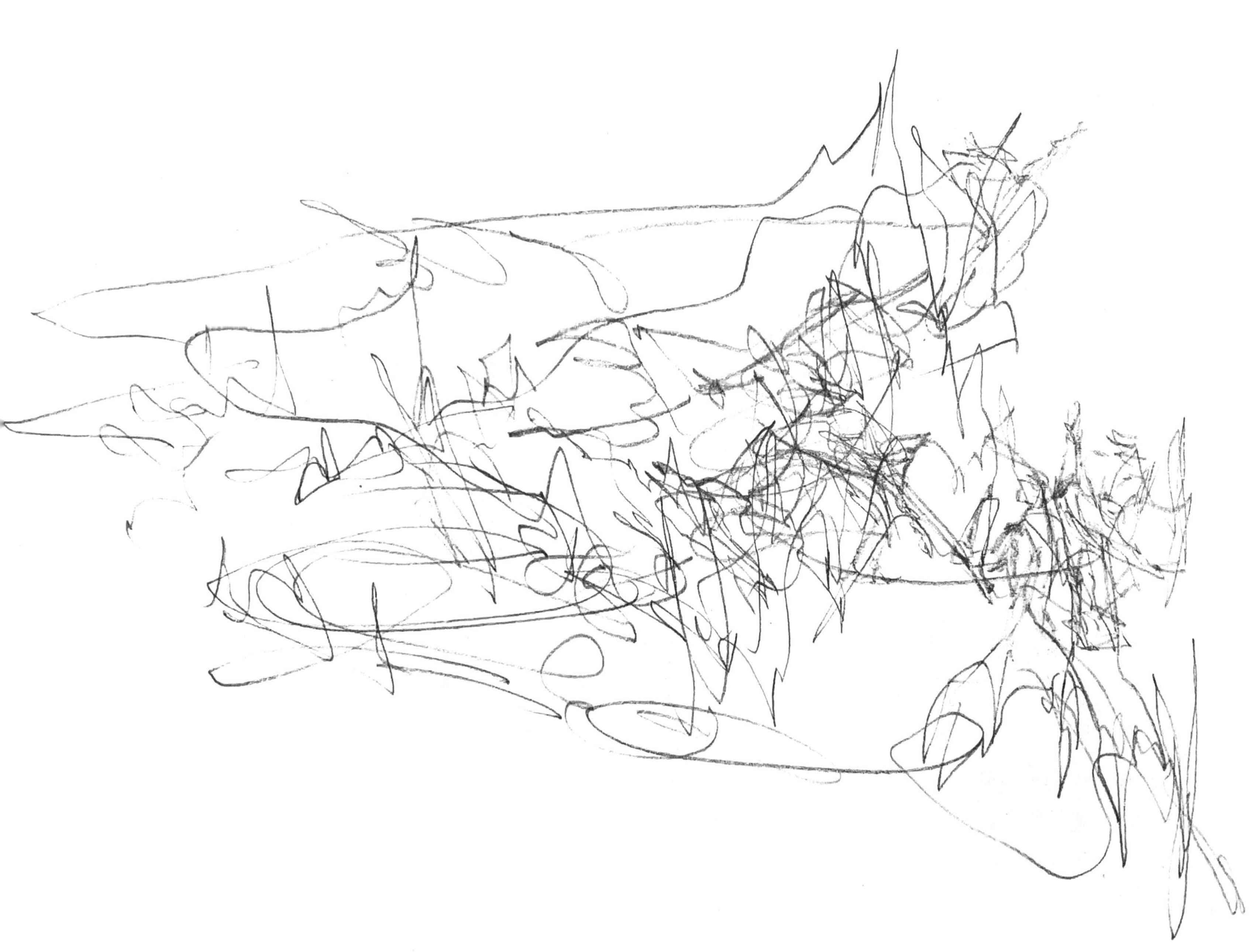

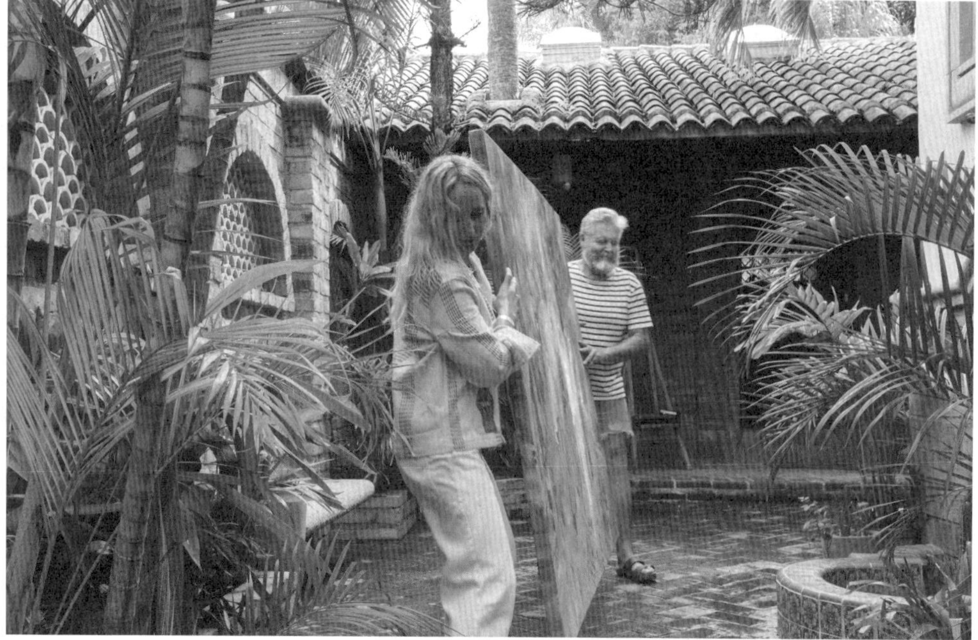

List of Works

Paintings

8
Jetsam*
2023
oil on linen
70 × 90" | 177.8 × 228.6 cm

12
Hold on Tight
2021
oil on linen
60 × 72" | 152.4 × 182.9 cm

16
Undertow*
2023
oil on linen
70 × 90" | 177.8 × 228.6 cm

20
Little Wild Bouquet*
2023
oil on linen
74 × 96" | 188 × 243.8 cm

26
Hippocampus
2023
oil on linen
60 × 80" | 152.4 × 203.2 cm

32
Metronome*
2023
oil on linen
80 × 96" | 203.2 × 243.8 cm

38
We met when we were almost young
2022
oil on linen
68¼ × 90¼" | 173.4 × 229.2 cm

42
Sea Change*
2023
oil on linen
2 panels, 74 × 96" | 188 × 243.8 cm
each
148 × 96" | 375.9 × 243.8 cm
overall

50
Montserrat
2023
oil on linen
60 × 72" | 152.4 × 182.9 cm

56
Pareidola
2023
oil on linen
74 × 96" | 188 × 243.8 cm

60
You into me, me into you
2023
oil on linen
74 × 96" | 188 × 243.8 cm

Drawings

89
Alexa*
2023
graphite on washi
12⅜ × 17" | 31.3 × 43.2 cm

90–91
Sara*
2023
graphite on cold pressed paper
9 × 12" | 22.9 × 30.5 cm

92–93
Megan*
2023
graphite on washi
12⅜ × 17" | 31.3 × 43.2 cm

94
Indiana*
2023
graphite on washi
12⅜ × 17" | 31.3 × 43.2 cm

95
Chun*
2023
graphite on washi
12⅜ × 17" | 31.3 × 43.2 cm

Published on the occasion of
Kylie Manning
Sea Change
March 26–May 9, 2024

Pace Gallery
12/F, H Queen's
80 Queen's Road Central
Hong Kong

Publication © 2024 Pace Publishing
Artworks by Kylie Manning © Kylie Manning

Text by Ted Barrow © 2024 Ted Barrow

Front cover, back cover, wrap, p. 1: *Undertow*, 2023 (detail)
pp. 6–7: *Little Wild Bouquet*, 2023 (detail)
p. 94: *You into me, me into you*, 2023 (detail)
p. 79: Kylie Manning in her studio, Queens, New York
pp. 80–88: New York City Ballet, *From You Within Me*, 2023
p. 96: Kylie and Tom Manning, Mexico

Photography:
Photo of New York City Ballet by Erin Baiano: pp. 80–88
Christopher Burke Studio: pp. 57–59, 61, 63–64
Courtesy The Collections of Kate Rothko Prizel and
Christopher Rothko: p. 66 (fig. 4)
Richard Gary: pp. 13–15, 74–75
Melissa Goodwin and Robyn Lehr Caspare: pp. 51, 53–54
Rich Lee: cover, pp. 1, 6–7, 9–11, 17–18, 21–23, 25, 27–30, 33–37,
42–43, 45–49
Erich Lessing / Art Resource, NY: p. 66 (fig. 5)
Tom Manning: p. 66 (figs. 2–3)
Pace Gallery: Still from *Kylie Manning on "From You Within Me."*
May 3, 2023, 7:02. p. 70 (fig. 9)
© The Metropolitan Museum of Art. Image source:
Art Resource, NY: p. 66 (fig. 1)
Jonathan Nesteruk: pp. 39, 41, 89–95
Alex Patrick: p. 96
Joe Perri: pp. 69 (fig. 6), 79
The Philadelphia Museum of Art / Art Resource, NY: p. 69 (fig. 8)
Elon Schoenholz: pp. 72–73, 76–77
© Worcester Art Museum / Bridgeman Images: p. 69 (fig. 7)

Design: Michael Dyer, Remake
Production: Paul Pollard
Editorial Director: Gillian Canavan
Editorial Manager: Madeline Gilmore
Rights & Reproductions: Vincent Wilcke
Color Separations: Altaimage, New York

Printing: Pristone, Singapore

ISBN: 978-1-948701-67-9
Library of Congress Control Number: 2023952329

Available through
ARTBOOK | D.A.P.
75 Broad Street, Suite 630
New York, NY 10004
www.artbook.com

* Included in the exhibition
Sea Change at Pace Gallery